LPGA's Guide to Every Shot

Ladies Professional Golf Association

Human Kinetics

Library of Congress Cataloging-in-Publication Data

LPGA's guide to every shot / Ladies Professional Golf Association
     p. cm.
  ISBN 0-88011-980-2
    1. Golf for women.   2. Swing (Golf)   I. Ladies Professional Golf Association.
  GV966.L64   2000
  796.352'3'082--dc21   99-089363

ISBN: 0-88011-980-2

Developmental Editor: Laura Hambly; **Assistant Editor**: Stephan Seyfert; **Copyeditor**: Bonnie Pettifor; **Proofreader**: Coree Schutter; **Permission Manager**: Cheri Banks; **Graphic Designer**: Nancy Rasmus; **Graphic Artist**: Sandra Meier; **Photo Editor**: Clark Brooks; **Cover Designer**: Jack W. Davis; **Photographer (cover)**: (top) © Rob Tringali/SportsChrome-USA; (bottom) Tom Roberts; **Photographer (interior)**: Tom Roberts, unless otherwise noted; photos on pages iii, 10, and 25 courtesy LPGA; photos on pages 38, 50, 62 (bottom), 117, 148, and 160 by Jeff Hornback, courtesy LPGA; photos on pages 71, 94, and 182 (bottom) by Jack Stohlman, courtesy LPGA; photo on page x courtesy Pia Nilsson; photo on page 13 courtesy Dana Rader; photos on pages 45 and 86 © Stephen Dunn/Allsport; photo on page 49 courtesy Lynn Marriott; photos on pages 56, 110 (bottom), 118, and 124 © Michael Cohen; photos on pages 62 (top) and 116 © Sport the Library/SportsChrome-USA; photos on pages 70, 72, 80, and 105 © Action Images; photos on pages 73 and 154 © Jean Higgins/ Unicorn Stock Photos; photo on page 77 courtesy Gale Peterson; photo on page 88 © David Cannon/ Allsport; photo on page 89 © Stephen Munday/Allsport; photo on page 93 courtesy Kay McMahon/ © Rick Sharp; photo on page 123 courtesy Sharon Miller; photo on page 135 courtesy Jane Frost; photo on page 159 courtesy Diane McHeffey

Human Kinetics books are available at special discounts for bulk purchase. Special editions or book excerpts can also be created to specification. For details, contact the Special Sales Manager at Human Kinetics.

Printed in Hong Kong   10   9   8   7   6   5   4   3   2   1

Human Kinetics
Web site: http://www.humankinetics.com/

United States: Human Kinetics
P.O. Box 5076, Champaign, IL 61825-5076
1-800-747-4457
e-mail: humank@hkusa.com

Canada: Human Kinetics
475 Devonshire Road Unit 100
Windsor, ON N8Y 2L5
1-800-465-7301 (in Canada only)
e-mail: humank@hkcanada.com

Europe: Human Kinetics
P.O. Box IW14, Leeds LS16 6TR
United Kingdom
+44 (0)113-278 1708
e-mail: humank@hkeurope.com

Australia: Human Kinetics
57A Price Avenue, Lower Mitcham
South Australia 5062
(08) 82771555
e-mail: liahka@senet.com.au

New Zealand: Human Kinetics
P.O. Box 105-231, Auckland Central
09-523-3462
e-mail: humank@hknewz.com

Dedicated to Dr. DeDe Owens,
LPGA master professional
and former LPGA tour player,
who shared her leadership skills and friendship,
but most importantly her love for people
and her knowledge and passion
for learning and teaching others.
The LPGA's proceeds from sales
of this book will be donated
to the Dr. DeDe Owens
Education and Research Fund.

1946–1999

Contents

A Note From the LPGA

LPGA's Guide to Every Shot is the first of the LPGA Academy Series books. Written for the new golfer as well as the experienced golfer, the book guides the reader from the pre-swing routine for all swings of the game to creating special shots to strategies for playing the game. The chapter sequence of the book is unique in that it begins with the foundation for all shots, the pre-swing, or address, routine and then applies those fundamentals to all the swings of the game from the green to the tee. The pre-swing routine is what sets up all swings of the game and is essential for creating consistently playable shots. Sixty-three percent of all shots in any game of golf are from 100 yards or less to the green, thus the focus is on the short game. Players often overlook the importance of these shots (putting, chipping, and pitching), yet clearly it is this part of the game that is the "scoring" game. The full swing, the most powerful swing of the game, is also necessary for success and demands a sound pre-swing routine to ensure distance and accuracy.

The format is also unique in that it uses both LPGA Tour professionals and LPGA teaching professionals working as a team to provide instructional models. All of the featured LPGA Tour members are multiple winners on the tour with four members in the LPGA Hall of Fame. The selected LPGA teaching professionals have all been recognized as LPGA National Teachers of the Year. The tour players and the teachers of the LPGA have teamed up to provide you with insights from learning to playing the game. The tour players are the models for each shot and provide on-course application and strategy, while the teaching professionals provide guidelines on how to learn and practice the shots.

The purpose of this book is to create a reference for learning the game of golf, beginning with swing fundamentals, explaining how to adapt swing fundamentals to create special shots, and concluding with strategies for playing the game. The presentation is user-friendly, allowing you to immediately apply the information to your game in a simple and successful way.

Dr. Betsy Clark
Director of Education, LPGA

Introduction

Discovering Your Potential

Teaching Professional: Pia Nilsson

From new golfers to professional players, each time a golfer steps onto the course she or he is trying to play her or his best game. The level they aspire to play may differ, but all players want to know how they can reach their potential. As coaches, too, we ask ourselves what we can do to help players improve their skills and play at the highest level possible.

What coaches and players must recognize is that all human beings are unique and therefore each one of us has a unique way of playing the game of golf. You can learn from others: Kelly Robbins's power, Liselotte Neumann's and Nancy Lopez's composure, Annika Sörenstam's patience . . . and so on. Remember, though, that you always need to make sure that it fits the way you are built, the way you think, the way you see things, your personality, your ambition level, your dreams, et cetera.

Although I have mostly worked with top-level golfers, I have found that all the following principles work equally well no matter what level you are playing at or what sport or occupation you are engaged in. In my role as a coach, I want to guide players in this process to find their unique approach to playing the game of golf.

I want players to be able to say "I"

- have a swing that suits me,
- practice in a way that fits me, my swing, and my play and results in achieving my goals,
- play a type of ball and clubs that fit me and my game,
- play my practice round in such a way that I learn what I need to learn about the course,
- have a physique that keeps me healthy and able to play the golf I want,
- have a diet that keeps me healthy and gives me the nutrition I need to perform my best,

- am able to listen to signals within me, and if something doesn't feel right, I know what I can do to regain my balance so that the necessary conditions exist for playing my best shot,
- am motivated in what I do,
- believe in what I do, and
- have clear objectives.

Becoming Your Own Best Coach

I believe in coaching players to become their own best coaches. Coaching yourself is a huge advantage because you always have yourself around! In a way, my goal as a coach is not to be needed. Instead, I want to focus the players' attention on things they can influence and then help them do something about it.

Liselotte Neumann and Annika Sörenstam are two excellent examples of Swedes who have found their own ways of doing things and are able to coach themselves to a very high degree. I have followed and coached Annika since she was on the Swedish Junior Team. What is it that makes her perform at such a high level? These are some areas that may not be visible watching Annika play on television, but that I think contribute highly to her success:

- Annika's ambition level is very high, and she has dreamt of and imaged herself being a world class player. At the same time, Annika has a balance in life and her "golf identity" is not all that she is. Who she is outside the golf course allows her to have strong self-esteem that is not totally dependent on her golf performance.

- Annika constantly wants to improve. No matter how she performs, she likes to keep on striving to get better. She focuses her attention on things she can influence and takes full responsibility for her actions. How I, as a player, interpret what happens to me on the golf course and in life, I believe makes a huge difference. Annika has a way of doing this that is simple and constructive: What do I do well and what is working? What can I improve on? How am I going to do it?

- Annika is very honest with herself as she is playing. She can sense if she is nervous, angry, or not motivated. She admits it, and she has tools within herself to coach herself out of a state that is not helping her golf game.

- Annika is very stubborn, in a positive way, and if she wants to improve any part of her game, she keeps at it until she feels she has got it. If what she is doing doesn't work, she will keep on adjusting until she finds a way that works for her.

Discovering Your Inherent Abilities

I believe that human beings have unlimited potential. What is needed for you to access a greater percentage of your ability than you do at present? I believe you have all the abilities you need. As a coach, I am like a catalyst for the player to discover and develop these abilities. For example, no player lacks mental strength or certain strokes. They are there within you. But, perhaps, they have not yet emerged. Perhaps you need to practice more or differently, change your habits or perspective, be more balanced, or the like. I will always believe that you can manage to do so if only you want to and are ready to work at it. When you perform at golf, you always get a result. For me, judging that result as success or failure is not particularly constructive. The interpretation is of utmost importance. Either the performance tells you that what you are doing is leading you toward your goals or it is not. If it isn't, the most important thing is to acknowledge it and make some sort of change. It is in this process that we learn a lot, if we choose to see it that way! I believe that tour players have the potential to shoot 54 on an 18-hole golf course. Nobody has done it yet, but I believe the capacity is within them.

Developing as a Human Being

I believe that the game of golf is a great metaphor for life. Many life skills are inherent in the game. As you play you have a wonderful opportunity to learn about yourself; experience qualities of life like courage, honesty, patience, and courtesy; be in nature; compete; be with friends; and manage challenges. I want my players and myself to develop as human beings through the game of golf. I want my approach to result in getting the ball in the hole in fewer strokes than before. In doing this, I want to be clear about the process. I want a process that produces a consistently successful result and that also produces the most positive experience for you as a human being. Short-term success can be achieved by cheating, doping, "dictatorial" leadership, threats, ignoring how you feel, and so on. These are approaches I cannot accept. The vision to develop as a human being through the game of golf is like a tuning fork and a reminder to us that you are a human being that plays golf and not a golfer who happens to be a human being. For me, the person is always more important than the result on the scorecard. At the same time, it is an approach that I feel leads to the very best performance. Nevertheless, I, as a person, am holding the club. The more I get to know myself and develop the qualities I want, the better my prospects of performing well. Golf requires that you play well even when the mood, muscles, coordination, attitude, and other factors are not what you would desire. You need to be able to discover that, acknowledge it, and then coach yourself into an optimal state of being to be able to perform. An example of a quality that most of us develop through playing golf at a high level is patience. A certain amount of patience is needed to get through all the incalculable challenges in the game. At the same time, patience is a quality that is equally, if not more, valuable in all areas of life.

These are some of the "backbone" ideas of my coaching. Keep on enjoying this wonderful game of ours; in the following pages, you can get the best advice in the world for your unique game.

Pia Nilsson was the 1998 European Solheim Cup Captain, the 1996 Swedish Sport Coach of the Year, and received a medal in 1998 from the king of Sweden for her leadership in sports. She won eight victories on the Swedish Golf Tour and won the Swedish Order of Merit in 1989. Pia played on the LPGA Tour from 1983 to 1987. She coached the Swedish National Women's Teams from 1990 to 1995 and the Swedish National Teams from 1996 to 1998. Pia is currently the Senior Head Coach for the Swedish National Teams.

PART I

Mastering Swings for Basic Shots

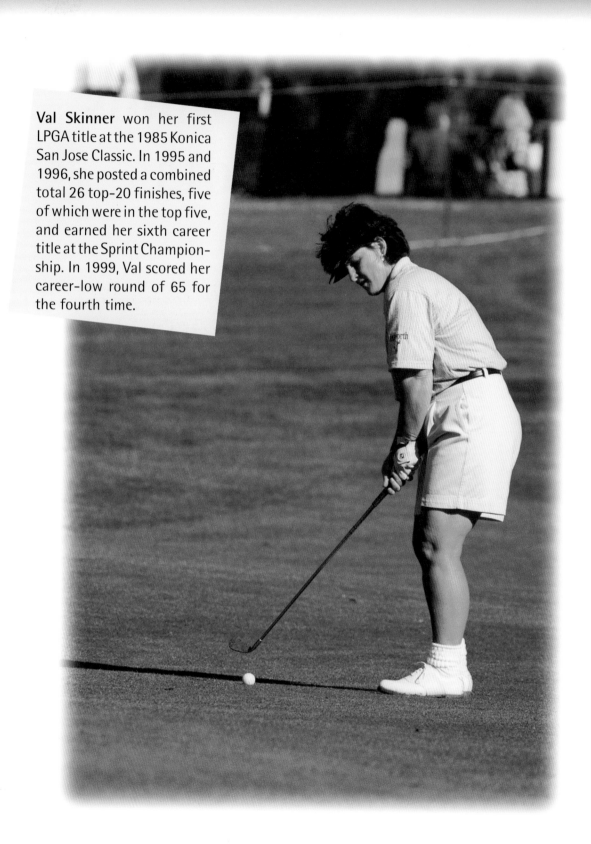

Val Skinner won her first LPGA title at the 1985 Konica San Jose Classic. In 1995 and 1996, she posted a combined total 26 top-20 finishes, five of which were in the top five, and earned her sixth career title at the Sprint Championship. In 1999, Val scored her career-low round of 65 for the fourth time.

Pre-Swing

Tour Professional: Val Skinner
Teaching Professional: Dana Rader

| Hand placement | Stance | Ball position | Aim |

As you watch the LPGA Tour professionals, they appear methodical as they prepare to hit each shot. Their approach—from the placement of their hands on the club to the position of the ball in their stance—is routine. Inconsistency in the pre-swing is like rolling the dice. The element of chance is introduced into your game at a much higher percentage as your pre-swing fundamentals, including how you hold the club, your posture, your stance, ball position, and aim and alignment, begin to vary. How you set up determines how you swing. In fact, as much as 95 percent of your inefficient swings are caused by the start position. This chapter shows you how to master the pre-swing fundamentals for consistency in all your shots and lower game scores. Take a 7 iron and work on your setup as we guide you through the fundamentals.

Hand Placement

TARGET HAND

First, place your target hand on the club so the back of your hand faces the target. Position the club so that the handle runs diagonally across your palm and fingers, then close your hand around the club. Your index finger and thumb should form an imaginary "V" that points between your chin and rear shoulder.

The club handle should run diagonally from the middle crease of the index finger to beneath the heel pad.

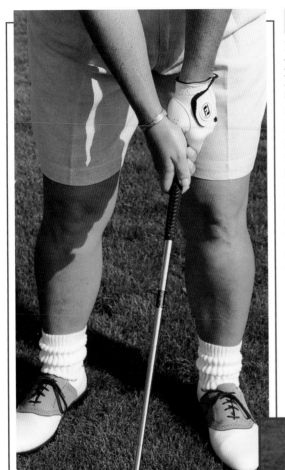

REAR HAND

Hold the club in front of you with your target hand, then extend your rear hand as though you are shaking hands. The palm of your rear hand should face the target. Place your rear hand on the club so the little finger of the hand rests on the index finger of your target hand. Your thumb should lie just to the target side of the club. Your index finger and thumb should again form an imaginary "V" that runs parallel to the "V" of the target hand. This is traditionally called the overlap grip.

The lifeline of the rear hand should be on top of the handle and target thumb.

Stance

Set your feet about shoulder-width apart and balance your weight evenly from side to side and front to back. For correct posture, bend from the hips and allow your arms to hang relaxed under your shoulders. Flex your knees slightly and balance your weight between the midsteps and balls of your feet.

The purpose of an efficient stance and posture is to establish the optimum position for swinging the club along the desired target line at impact.

Ball Position

Ball position varies slightly, depending on a player's skill level and the intent of the shot, which is discussed in later chapters. In general, position the ball in the center of your stance for wedges through 5 iron. For 4 iron through 2 iron and woods, position the ball slightly forward of center to the inside of your target heel.

Wedges through 5 iron.

4 iron through 2 iron and woods.

Aim and Alignment

"Aim and alignment" refer to the placement of the clubface and your body in relation to the intended target. First aim the club to the target, then align your body (feet, hips, and shoulders) parallel to the target line. Picture yourself standing on a railroad track:

- The ball and club are on the outer track, or "target line," that goes to the target.
- The club forms a "T" with the track.
- The inside track is parallel to the target line. Align your heels, hips, and shoulders parallel to the target line.

VAL SKINNER'S PRE-SWING STRATEGY

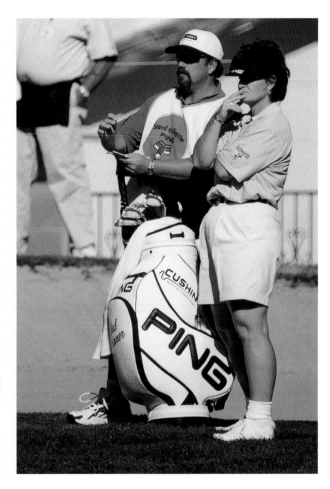

When I arrive at the ball, I analyze all the variables. Starting from behind the ball, I find my target for the shot. I decide where to land the ball to leave myself the best opportunity to make the next shot. This process helps to create the visual picture of the shot I want to hit. The next picture then creates a feel for the shot. At that point, I simply start to react to my target. I go through my setup routine: see my target in my mind's eye, feel the swing just thinking of the target, and then pull the trigger.

In my setup routine, I first get behind the ball and pick a spot a foot in front of the ball and in line with my target. I visualize an imaginary line from the ball through the spot along the intended target line. Next, I visualize where I want to set my feet, hips, and shoulders so they are parallel to that line. If I line up properly, I should be able to rotate my head toward the target and comfortably look at it. If I have to look over my shoulder, I'm too far right. If I have to look up and out, I'm too far left.

I work hard at repeating a good routine—a physical, mental, and strategical routine. It is important to stay in a relaxed state of being under pressure.

PRE-SWING CONFIDENCE BRINGS VICTORY

It was 1985. I was looking over a 30-foot-high pine tree from 155 yards. If I could hit the 6 iron high right over the top of that pine, I would win my first LPGA tournament. If I could leave that 6 iron shot below the hole, I could make the putt and beat Hall-of-Famer Pat Bradley in a playoff. Wow! What a great time to react.

I knew the key was to stay confident in my approach. Being confident in preparation leads to confidence in my swing. I went through my setup routine: see, feel, and go.

Well, I didn't make the putt, but par was good enough for the win and my first trophy.

KEY DRILLS FOR MASTERING THE PRE-SWING

Hand Placement Drill

To practice holding the club, try positioning your hands on the club with your eyes closed. Then open your eyes and see if your hands are in the proper position. You can practice this anywhere—at home or the office.

Posture Drill

To establish the desired feeling for posture do the following:

1. Stand sideways to a mirror.
2. Place a golf club on your back, touching the back of your head with one end and your tailbone with the other end.
3. Flex your knees slightly, and then bow forward, keeping the two ends of the shaft touching your head and tailbone. Tilt over to approximately 45 degrees.

   You know you've hit the correct position when

   • your hips feel like they are farther back than usual,
   • your weight feels balanced between your midsteps and the balls of your feet, and
   • your arms feel relaxed with no tension from rounding your shoulders.

Aiming Drill

At home or during practice, use three extra clubs to help you aim:

1. Align two parallel clubs to the target line, leaving a space between them. Place a ball in the space. Take your setup position. Then place one club just behind your heels and parallel to the target line clubs.
2. Practice your alignment without hitting balls. Use this station frequently to feel and visualize your desired address position.

PRE-SWING SUCCESS CHECKLIST

✔ Good golf starts with the hands. The hands are the only connection you have with a golf club, and what you do with your hands equals what happens to the clubface. An effective hold on the club is critical to playable shots in golf. Note the use of "effective" rather than "comfortable." These terms may not initially match. Through better understanding and practice, however, they will.

✔ Think of your stance as a platform, or base. Having a platform allows you to maintain your balance to generate power while maintaining muscular, or athletic, readiness.

✔ Professionals appear confident and committed as they approach each shot, prepared to execute. This is not by chance! It is through practice, commitment, and belief. When you are confident in preparation, confidence in your swing is a product. Your mind and body are in sync. The resulting swing motion of each shot and your game develop a pattern that is predictable. You can be imaginative and creative, playing the whole game with a solid foundation.

SUMMARY

Golf is a target game. The consistency of your pre-swing fundamentals allows you to play golf with target awareness, with your club and body set to create the shot results you desire. You are in control of your consistency. You can literally practice your pre-swing routine anywhere and anytime. Imagine, you can be on the road to lower scores with just a few minutes of practice. Lowering your scores will come with consistency in your foundation, the pre-swing fundamentals.

The pre-swing fundamentals relate to every swing you make. Remember, your pre-swing fundamentals create your routine for success:

1. Determine your desired target.
2. Place your hands on the club consistently for the desired shot.
3. Take dead aim through consistent aiming and alignment of your club and body relative to your intended target.
4. Set your posture relative to the club you are using and the desired shot.
5. Establish a consistent ball position for the desired shot.

There will be slight variations in your pre-swing fundamentals as you learn partial shots and specialty shots. However, the basics you have learned here will be with you for a lifetime.

Dana Rader turned professional in 1980 and was honored in 1990 as the LPGA's National Teacher of the Year. In 1996 and 1999, she was named one of the Top 100 Teachers in the United States by *Golf Magazine*. She received the Top 25 Women in Business Achievement award by *The Business Journal* in 1998. Dana has written for many leading publications, appears regularly on the Golf Channel, and serves on the advisory board for Nancy Lopez Golf. She is the Director of Golf at Ballantyne Resort's Golf Club in Charlotte, North Carolina.

Jane Crafter won the 1978 New Zealand Amateur and the 1980 Belgian Amateur and represented Australia in international competition 10 times before moving to the United States and turning professional. She won the 1992 and 1996 Australian Ladies Masters and the 1997 Australian Women's Open. Jane captured her first LPGA victory in 1990.

2

Putt

Tour Professional: Jane Crafter
Teaching Professional: Dr. Betsy Clark

Putting accounts for approximately 50 percent of the strokes in determining par for a course. Yet, it is the most neglected aspect of practice. As a new golfer or experienced player, the putt is one of the most important shots of the game. It's the shortest swing, but still the shot that many are challenged by. If the putt is 50 percent of your game strokes, consider spending about that much of your practice time as a new golfer learning the putt. If you are an experienced golfer, think about how you spend most of your practice time—hitting full shots or working on your short game? Now think about the number of putts under three feet that you have missed during a round or that you have seen missed during play with your friends and by the pros on television. That three-foot putt has the same value as a long drive or precise iron shot to the green.

How to Putt

SETUP

You need to slightly modify the setup position described in chapter 1. Modify the triangle formed by your arms and shoulders to accommodate the shorter and more upright design of putters. Your arms should be comfortably bent. Adjust your posture also, keeping your hands in line with your shoulders and setting your head and eyes over the ball on the target line. This adjustment enhances your control of the shorter, more precise stroke. Place your hands down on the putter handle for control, maintaining light hand pressure. Position the ball to the target side of center.

Some players prefer to use a target hand low grip, rather than the more conventional overlap grip.

SWING

The putting stroke follows a pendular motion, with the backswing and forward swing being equal. Move your hands, arms, and club as a unit to create a constant pace throughout the swing. Keeping your hands light will enhance a steady, quiet body throughout the swing. The length of your backswing and speed of the swing governs the length of the putt.

Target hand low grip.

How to Putt

CONTACT

Keep the putter blade low to the ground so that it stays on the intended target line. During the stroke, keep your upper and lower body still. The lighter you hold the putter, the easier to keep your body still. Swing *through* the ball, focusing on a smooth back-and-through motion.

Target hand low grip.

FOLLOW-THROUGH

The putter face moves through the ball on the intended line (path) of the putt toward the target. The follow-through is what controls the direction of the putt.

Target hand low grip.

JANE CRAFTER'S PUTTING STRATEGY

As I approach the green, I always look at its general slope. I look to see if it slopes back to front, front to back, right to left, or left to right. I also look at the type of grass—Bermuda or bent—as these factors influence the direction and speed of the ball.

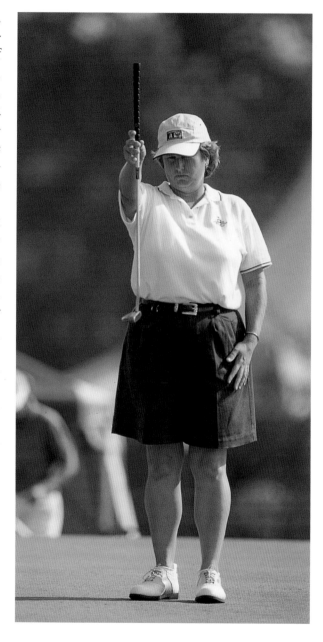

After I study what slopes are between my ball and the hole, I pace off the exact length of the putt. This gives me a reference for the length of the putt and the speed needed to get the putt to the hole. I practice different lengths of putts on the practice green beforehand to get a feel for the speed of the greens for the day. I like to look at each putt from behind the hole, to survey accurately both the break and the speed. Putting is a function of both the target line and pace. You cannot judge the line without considering the speed or pace of the putt.

Before stepping up to the putt, I take two rehearsal strokes. I also take a moment to visualize the putt—from the setup of the shot to the cheering of the crowd after the ball goes in. During the actual stroke, I try to reproduce my rehearsal stroke. I try not to think about results, like what it would mean to make or miss the shot. If the shot goes in, I feel satisfied that my goal was achieved. If not, I analyze what went wrong. Perhaps it hit a bump, or I did not make a good mechanical stroke, or my mental focus was off. I try not to put any undo pressure on myself, but instead look for something I can improve next time.

PUTTING TO WIN THE 1996 AUSTRALIAN LADIES MASTERS

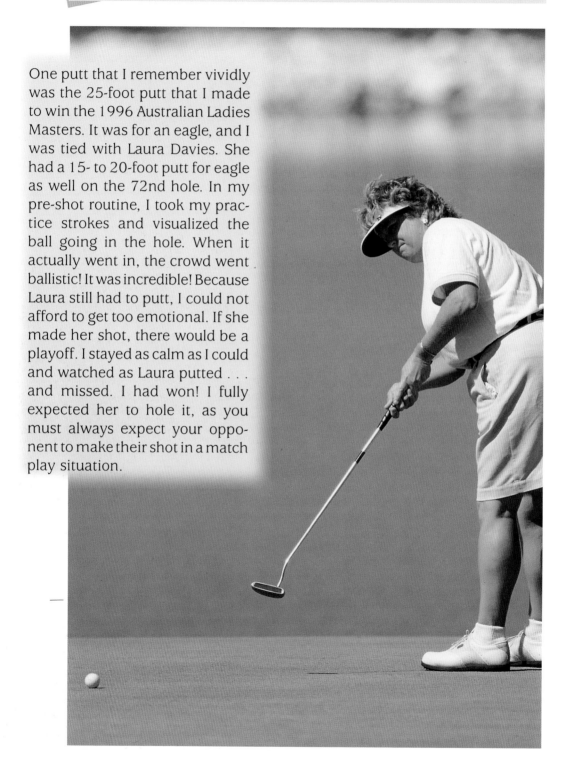

One putt that I remember vividly was the 25-foot putt that I made to win the 1996 Australian Ladies Masters. It was for an eagle, and I was tied with Laura Davies. She had a 15- to 20-foot putt for eagle as well on the 72nd hole. In my pre-shot routine, I took my practice strokes and visualized the ball going in the hole. When it actually went in, the crowd went ballistic! It was incredible! Because Laura still had to putt, I could not afford to get too emotional. If she made her shot, there would be a playoff. I stayed as calm as I could and watched as Laura putted . . . and missed. I had won! I fully expected her to hole it, as you must always expect your opponent to make their shot in a match play situation.

KEY DRILLS FOR PUTTING

Railroad Drill

Place two clubs like a railroad track, three to four feet from the hole on a straight putt. Practice putting between the tracks to develop alignment and swing path. Repeat this drill for 10 to 15 minutes, then remove the clubs and continue to work on a variety of lengths, using one ball and your pre-swing routine each time.

Stroke Drill

This drill works on stroke trust and helps you develop a sense of patience in your stroke. Using one ball, select various distances to practice. Go through your pre-swing routine with each putt. Prior to the stroke, shut your eyes and putt. From the stroke, predict the outcome (e.g., made, long, short, right, or left) before opening your eyes. This is a fun partner drill.

Steadiness Drill

If you have problems moving on putts or tend to be jerky in your motion, set a club against your target leg while putting. If the club drops, your lower body has moved too much. Lighten up your hand pressure and continue practicing putts of various distances until the club remains steady during the stroke.

PUTTING SUCCESS CHECKLIST

✔ Read the green before every shot. Find a spot behind your ball directly in line with the hole, then bend down so you can see the slope of the green. If the slope is higher on one side, the ball will curve to the lower side. Reading the green is necessary for aiming. Oftentimes you will not aim at the hole but rather at a spot inches away from the hole because of the slope or curvature of the green.

✔ Determine your line. Set the putter head square to the target by placing the putter blade at a right angle to the intended line of the putt.

✔ Take a few practice swings to feel your distance.

✔ Putting is a "quiet swing" with a smooth, continuous stroke. Follow a pendular motion and maintain a constant pace from beginning to end.

SUMMARY

Putting is the most important part of the golf game, as it can make or break your score and, consequently, your psyche. The emphasis in putting is on short distance, accuracy, control, and direction. It is the least complex of all golf swings. It is not hard to learn the basics of putting, and with some concerted practice, you can become a good putter. Most important is convincing yourself that you *will* become a good putter and being determined to work to that end. If you think you can't, you won't, and if you think you can, you will.

Dr. Betsy Clark was named director of education for the LPGA in 1992, after having worked in the golf industry since 1974. As an area consultant for more than 10 years with the National Golf Foundation, she conducted numerous player development clinics and teacher/coach workshops throughout the country. Betsy is an accomplished writer for various golf industry publications as well as a committee member for numerous association initiatives. A Class A member of the LPGA Teaching and Club Professional Division since 1984, she was voted LPGA National Teacher of the Year in 1991.

Colleen Walker won her first professional tournament title in 1987 at the Mayflower Classic. In 1988, she earned the Vare Trophy and placed in the top 10 in three of the four major championships. Colleen won her first major championship at the 1997 du Maurier Classic. She has nine total career victories.

3

Chip Shot

Tour Professional: Colleen Walker
Teaching Professional: Dr. Betsy Clark

The chip shot is like a long putt except that you loft the ball for the first few feet, then it rolls. However, it still uses more ground time than air time. Like putting, the emphasis is on short distance, accuracy, control, and direction.

The chipping technique is very versatile with multiple options from very low run shots to higher shots over bunkers. You can use it from the fringe of the green to as far back as your control allows. Select the chip shot when the distance is easily within your control, and the ball has distance to roll. The chip shot is the simplest and most accurate approach shot because it uses the fewest moving body parts. It is a safer shot than the pitch shot, because it is a shorter, more compact motion. If the conditions allow you to select either a pitch shot or chip shot, select the chip shot.

How to Chip

SETUP

The stance is narrow, with your feet less than shoulder-width apart and your hips and feet slightly open. Position the ball in the center of your stance. Lean your upper body over the target leg, as though you are looking at the target side of the ball. Position your hands slightly in front of the ball, off your target leg. Tilt the shaft toward the target so that the handle leads the clubhead.

Your shoulders should be parallel to the intended target line. Together, your arms and shoulders should form a comfortable extended triangle.

SWING

As with the putt, the triangle formed by your arms and shoulders should swing as one unit, like a pendulum. Your wrists should stay firm and quiet, with little to no movement. The length and speed of the swing determine distance.

Your lower body should remain quiet throughout the swing.

How to Chip

CONTACT

Maintain the pendular back-and-through motion and swing *through* the ball. Contact is crisp, with the ball contacting the center of the clubface.

Minimize your weight shift during the backswing and forward swing.

FOLLOW-THROUGH

Brush the grass with the leading edge of the club, keeping the clubface aimed at the intended line.

Hold the follow-through position to check your balance. Your weight should be on your target leg.

COLLEEN WALKER'S CHIPPING STRATEGY

The strategy of the shot is basically just to get the ball over the fringe and then let it roll to the hole as if it was a putt. When you try to putt from the fringe, the ball sometimes comes off higher grass, which can kick it off-line. However, the chip shot lets you get the ball over that fringe and onto the green, where it rolls pretty much in a true line.

Club selection for the chip shot depends on what the distance is between the ball and the hole. I use a pitching wedge to a 6 iron, depending on that distance. Most of the time if the greens are really, really fast, I either use a pitching wedge or 9 iron. Again, it also depends on the slope of the green.

A RECORD NUMBER OF CHIP-INS

The chip shot is valuable in that you can use it from any distance—30, 40, 50, 60 feet. I just vary my club selection, depending on the distance.

The most chip-ins I have had in one year is 19. As far as having chipped in to win a golf tournament, I have not, but 19 chip-ins is probably the most ever out here on tour.

AP/Wide World Photos

KEY DRILLS FOR CHIPPING

Variable Lie Drill

Using one ball, chip and putt from 10 spots around the green. Imagine you are on the course, and the shot has meaning. In other words, imagine that this very shot could clinch the win. With each shot, change the distance and lie of the ball. As needed, also change the club. Use a more-lofted club for a chip shot needing less distance and roll and a less-lofted club for a chip shot needing more distance and roll. Maintain your focus on the target. Be sure your club selection matches the shot requirements. Keep track of your "up and downs"(chips and one-putts) so that you learn what your strengths and weaknesses are and know what to focus on.

Ladder Drill

In your practice area, place five or six clubs in a row like rungs on a ladder, each six feet apart. Practice chipping with the goal of landing the ball between the spaces. This drill will help you begin to visualize the trajectory and carry distance of your chips when varying the length of your backswing and using different clubs.

Cluster Drill

This drill is designed to help you develop a feel for chipping from various distances. Around a green, select a club and five balls. Chip the first ball. Your goal is to chip the next four balls in a cluster around the first ball. Change clubs and distances. This is an excellent drill to use before playing to get a feel for your stroke and the speed of the greens.

Along-the-Track Drill

From about five feet off the practice green, place two clubs about two feet apart in a track toward the intended target. Chip balls from within the track, keeping the club moving back and through along the track toward the target.

Chip and Putt Drill

Play a chip and putt course around the green. Using one ball, start from off the green, chip to a target on the putting green, and putt out. Set up from nine different points around the fringe or just off the fringe, and see how many par 3s you can make.

Club-Swapping Drill

Chip 20 balls from the same spot to different targets around the green. Experiment with different clubs, seeing which clubs work best for different distances.

CHIPPING SUCCESS CHECKLIST

✔ Anticipate roll. Visualize the outcome: ball pops up, lands, and rolls. Imagine where the ball needs to land to roll to the target.

✔ When selecting a club for your chip shot, consider the following: lower irons (5, 6, 7) will create more roll and less loft whereas using higher irons (8, 9, wedges) will result in more loft and less roll.

✔ Base your club selection on the following:
   Distance from the green, how much fairway or fringe you have to chip over
   Lie of the ball
   Distance from the flagstick
   Roll desired

✔ When in a situation where you could chip or pitch, chip. It is a higher-percentage shot and more versatile in club selection and assorted lie conditions.

SUMMARY

The proper pre-swing technique is vital to executing a good chip shot. Slightly modifying the setup position—moving your hands down on the club, maintaining a narrow stance, leaving your hips and feet open, placing your weight on the target side—will help you create the desired trajectory. Because the chip shot is a shorter, more compact motion, it is not hard to master the proper technique. All it takes is confidence, a consistent pre-swing routine, and a little practice!

Dr. Betsy Clark was named director of education for the LPGA in 1992, after having worked in the golf industry since 1974. As an area consultant for more than 10 years with the National Golf Foundation, she conducted numerous player development clinics and teacher/coach workshops throughout the country. Betsy is an accomplished writer for various golf industry publications as well as a committee member for numerous association initiatives. A Class A member of the LPGA Teaching and Club Professional Division since 1984, she was voted LPGA National Teacher of the Year in 1991.

Hollis Stacy claimed her first 3 professional career wins in 1977, including her first U.S. Women's Open title. She won it again in 1978 and 1984 and became one of four women to have claimed the title three or more times. Hollis earned at least one victory each season from 1977 through 1985. She owns 18 career victories, including four majors.

4

Pitch Shot

Tour Professional: Hollis Stacy
Teaching Professional: Lynn Marriott

The pitch shot is one of the most frequently used shots by all golfers. Consider your average round. Do you hit all the greens in regulation? Do you hit all the par 5s in two? Rarely! The pitch shot has the greatest variability of distance, from 80-plus yards to next to the fringe. This is an extremely important shot to your game.

Use the pitch shot to hit a high trajectory into the green, with very little ball roll upon landing. The pitch is necessary when the distance from the green will not allow a lower run shot or there is a need to carry the ball over an obstacle or bunker. This shot's main intent, however, is not one of distance, but more of accuracy with distance control.

How to Pitch

SETUP

The main difference in the setup of the pitch shot from the description in chapter 1 is in the width of your stance. The pitch shot uses a narrow stance, with your feet less than shoulder-width apart and slightly open.

SWING

To keep the focus on accuracy and control, rather than distance, the length of the backswing tends to be shorter—one-half to three-quarters that of the full swing. The narrow stance makes it easier to execute a shorter, more vertical swing, which controls distance and creates a higher trajectory.

How to Pitch

CONTACT

At contact, your weight should be on your target leg with your rear knee turned toward your target knee.

FOLLOW-THROUGH

The swing continues smoothly through the position shown here until your hands reach slightly higher than your target shoulder. Your hips should naturally turn toward the target.

HOLLIS STACY'S PITCHING STRATEGY

When it comes to ball flight, I like to hit pitch shots at a bit lower trajectory, because I feel like I can control the distance better and the wind won't bother it that much. I control ball flight with the position of the ball in my stance. A bit to the target side of center is where I like hitting my pitch shot. If I want to hit it lower, I'll move it back an inch; if I want to hit it higher, I'll play it up, more toward the target foot.

Usually, my basic pitch shot will have two or three hops, and that's it. I won't allow for any backspin, because I think backspin is a deterrent to hitting balls close.

When I'm faced with the choice between a basic pitch shot and a basic chip shot, I actually prefer the basic chip. If I have a 30-yard pitch, for example, I prefer hitting past 15 yards. To me, anything short of that requires lots of practice, touch, and more knowledge of the green.

CONQUERING A DIFFICULT PITCH SHOT

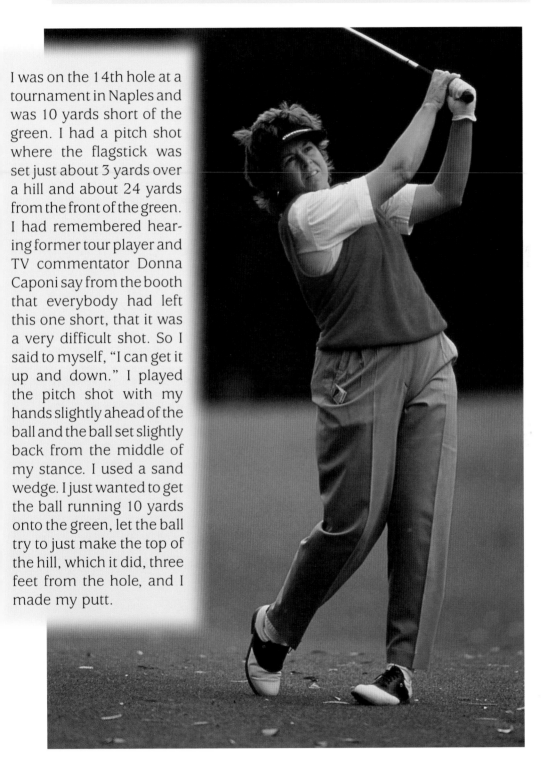

I was on the 14th hole at a tournament in Naples and was 10 yards short of the green. I had a pitch shot where the flagstick was set just about 3 yards over a hill and about 24 yards from the front of the green. I had remembered hearing former tour player and TV commentator Donna Caponi say from the booth that everybody had left this one short, that it was a very difficult shot. So I said to myself, "I can get it up and down." I played the pitch shot with my hands slightly ahead of the ball and the ball set slightly back from the middle of my stance. I used a sand wedge. I just wanted to get the ball running 10 yards onto the green, let the ball try to just make the top of the hill, which it did, three feet from the hole, and I made my putt.

KEY DRILLS FOR PITCHING

Steady Swing Drill

Maintaining balance is vital to the pitch shot. A simple way to enhance stability is to practice with a doorstop wedged under the outside middle of each foot. The wedge prevents your knees and hips from sliding laterally and forces the muscles in your hips, back, and shoulders to turn to create the proper arm swing.

Wrist Motion Drill

Practice the pitch swing without a ball. Place a tee in the hole in the end of your golf club grip. Practice taking pitch swings back and through from hip-to-hip length. With proper wrist-hinging, the tee should point to the ground on the backswing, stopping at hip level, and, on the forward swing, finishing at hip level.

Now practice with a ball. With a pitching wedge, sand wedge, or 9 iron, place a wooden tee in the hole in the grip end of the club. Hit balls toward targets placed at 20, 40, and 60 yards. Check for the tee to be pointing to the ground at the backswing and the forward swing.

Toss Drill

A drill that will help you get a feel for pitch shot distance as well as arm and hand position on the swing is to actually toss balls underhanded to a green. Stand sideways to the target as when swinging with a club, and toss balls underhanded. Start with a five-yard shot and gradually increase distance in five-yard increments until you are tossing balls from your maximum throwing distance. The tendency is to stand flat-footed. Allow you lower body to turn through the tossing motion as the distance increases. This motion mirrors the pitch.

Pitch and Hole-Out Drill

Pitch one ball at a time to the flag. Then walk up and hole-out the putt. This is realistic practice and makes each shot and putt important. This drill is more game-like than the others and so it is good to end your practice session with it.

The Wedges Drill

The pitch shot is typically executed with a pitching wedge, lob wedge, or a sand wedge. Experiment and practice with all wedges to find out which club works best for you at various target distances from 20 yards to 100 yards. Full swings are always easier to execute than partial swings, even with the wedge. Find out the maximum or full pitch shot distance for each of your wedges by taking 10 or 12 comfortable, full swings with each wedge and then pacing the distance of each cluster of shots. The more you know about your wedges and what they can do for you, the more confident you will be with the pitch shots.

PITCHING SUCCESS CHECKLIST

✔ Club selection allows you to control the distance and the trajectory. Use the most-lofted clubs—9 iron, pitching wedge, sand wedge, and lob wedge. The lob wedge is particularly helpful if you have problems executing the 30- to 40-yard-high shots. Practice with more-lofted clubs to determine your distance control.

✔ Maintain a narrow stance so that it's easier to execute a shorter, more vertical swing. This, in turn, controls distance and creates a higher trajectory.

✔ For control, your swing motion should have a shortened backswing length—one-half to three-quarters that of the full swing.

✔ Place your hands lower on the club.

SUMMARY

The pitch shot is a partial swing, meaning the goal is accuracy and control rather than distance, as in the full swing. You can use the pitch shot anywhere from 10 to 90 yards from the green, depending on your skill. Because you can use it from such a wide range of distances, it is an important shot to every player's game. Success in the pitch shot lies primarily in the execution of proper setup, swing length, and pace. Practicing the pitch from different distances will enhance your control of this important stroke-saving shot.

Lynn Marriott is one of only six women listed as *Golf Magazine*'s Top 100 Instructors. She was named the LPGA National Teacher of the Year in 1992. Marriott is actively involved with The First Tee, a golf program for disadvantaged children. She has also worked as a consultant to the LPGA Urban Youth Golf Program. She has been a consultant to many top college programs and a contributing writer for *Golf for Women Magazine*, *Golf Magazine*, *Golf Tips Magazine*, and *AZ Golf Arizona Republic*. She has been a Class A member of the LPGA since 1982 and a Class A member of the PGA since 1984.

JoAnne Carner has won 42 LPGA events including two majors. She has received three Rolex Player of the Year awards, five Vare Trophies, and numerous other awards since joining the tour in 1970. She was inducted into the LPGA Hall of Fame in 1982 and became the 10th woman to be inducted into the World Golf Hall of Fame in 1985.

5

Sand Shot

Tour Professional: JoAnne Carner
Teaching Professional: Lynn Marriott

The sand bunker shot is the easiest—yet among the most feared—in golf. For years these shots were affectionately called *trap shots*, but the appropriate term is a *sand* or *bunker shot*. Lack of opportunities to practice the sand shot is the leading cause of fear, not the execution or technique of the shot.

There are three primary goals with any sand shot: (1) get out, (2) get on, and (3) get close. If you are in the "Bunker Anxiety Club," perhaps you are trying to get close when your goal should be to get out. If you consistently get out, you may need to elevate your goal to getting close. By giving yourself the biggest possible margin for error, you will start getting out of the sand more consistently, onto the green, and near the hole.

How to Hit Sand Shots

SETUP

Position your feet, hips, and shoulders so they are slightly open to the target. The ball position is forward of center in your open stance. Prior to placing your hands on the club, open the clubface slightly. Pick a spot on the sand an inch or two behind the ball. That is where you will want to "spank" the sand with your club.

Your weight should lean toward your target side.

SWING

Imagine you are making your pitch swing. Because the goal is to contact the sand first and not the ball, the ball will not go as far with the same swing length and pace as in the fairway. Control acceleration and distance by using the two-to-one ratio: if you have a 20-yard shot from the bunker to the flagstick, take a swing that matches at least a 40-yard pitch shot on grass.

Your weight shifts to your rear leg on the backswing.

How to Hit Sand Shots

CONTACT

Contact the sand first. The sand wedge has a wider and heavier bottom, or *sole*, and the club literally "splashes" the ball out of the sand.

You can contact the sand one to three inches behind the ball, and the ball will fly out of the sand *if* you continue to accelerate through the sand.

FOLLOW-THROUGH

Accelerate through the sand by making sure you finish your swing with your weight moving to the target side.

Your swing continues smoothly, and your hips turn to face the target during the follow-through phase.

JOANNE CARNER'S SAND SHOT STRATEGY

I've always felt that if you are a really good bunker player, you can hole these shots. However, most people fear bunker shots, and it's simply because they don't know how to play them. I attribute my success with bunker shots to understanding and practicing the technique—and having confidence in the shot.

The sand shot is different from your normal swing in that you have to squat a little more and drop your hands. I play my hands way down by my knees because it allows me to quickly break my wrist on the backswing. If you stand too tall in the bunker, you won't play a good bunker shot. A taller posture will limit the type of shots you can play, whereas if you squat a little more and keep your hands down, you can play a lot more shots.

The swing path of the club also differs from the regular swing. With the sand shot it's always outside the target line to inside with a very fast wrist break at the beginning of the shot.

One sand shot technique is to hit bunker shots as hard as you want. The more the pressure is on, the more I'll open the blade and hit just a little farther behind the ball and hit it hard. This helps relieve the tension that comes when I'm under pressure. For example, if it comes down to the last hole, and I've got to get it up and out of the sand to win the tournament, then I would open the shot a little more and hit it harder, higher, and shorter.

Once you learn the straightaway shots, I recommend practicing from different lies so that in a tournament or game, if you happen to be in a footprint, for example, you won't get anxious and give up on the shot. With practice, you'll know exactly what the ball is going to do when it comes out of the sand. You'll be in complete control!

A WINNING SAND SHOT

I was preparing to hit a bunker shot. It was about the 14th hole, and the pin was just below a double-tiered green, so it was going to be a tough shot. If I hit it too hard, I would get on that upper level and have a downhill putt, which would make it difficult. But if I hit it too soft, then the ball would be liable to roll back off the green. I decided to play a bank shot off the edge of the bunker up onto the green, fly it to the flagstick, and let it roll about three-quarters up the slope and then roll back down. I lipped the cup with the shot. It was a very important birdie because it allowed me to go on to win the tournament and amass my 35th win, which put me in the LPGA Hall of Fame.

KEY DRILLS FOR SAND SHOTS

Tee Drill

This drill will encourage you to allow the flange of the sand wedge to take a shallow cut of sand from under the ball, sending the ball out of the bunker onto the green. Place a ball on a tee in the sand. Push the tee into the sand so the ball is level with the sand. When you swing, let the sand wedge clip the tee out of the sand. The tee should fly out of the bunker and toward the hole.

Sand Pile Drill

To sense how much acceleration is required to execute a bunker shot, place a pile of sand just outside the practice bunker with a ball on top. Select a distance of about 30 yards. First make a pitch shot from the grass at that distance. Then, execute your shot from the pile of sand with the ball on top. Notice the degree of acceleration and length of swing needed from the sand compared to the grass.

Varying-the-Club Drill

A challenging and advanced drill is to hit bunker shots with different clubs: pitching wedge, 9, 7, and 5. Lay the clubface wide open and position the ball forward in your stance. Find out what kind of swing you must execute to hit the ball out of the sand. After this practice, a basic bunker shot is really easy!

Splash Drill

This is an acceleration drill to allow you to swing through the sand with enough pace to send the sand out of the bunker, which in turn sends the ball out. This drill uses the practice and experience you have gained from doing the first three drills. Draw an oval in the sand about the size of a dollar bill. Place a tee in the center of the oval. Your goal is to begin to feel the amount of acceleration necessary to land the ball specific distances:

- Splash sand from the bunker that lands on the first third of the green.
- Splash sand from the bunker that lands on the second third of the green.
- Splash sand from the bunker that lands on the back of the green.

SAND SHOT SUCCESS CHECKLIST

Preparation through practice will help you improve your bunker "attitude"—and get you out of the sand. The following are key points to remember:

✔ Know your goal from the sand.

✔ Your address position is absolutely key. Feet, hips, and shoulders are slightly open, with the clubface aligned to the target. Ball position is forward of center. Your weight should lean slightly toward the target.

✔ Use your pitch swing technique learned in chapter 4 with the two-to-one ratio for distance control.

✔ Contact the sand first. Your sand wedge was designed specifically to slide through the sand without digging in too deeply, taking a thin cut of sand. The ball rides out with the sand.

✔ Hit the green-side bunker shot when in the following situations:

  Green-side bunkers

  Deep rough around the green

  Fairway bunkers when close to a high lip and the objective is to get out

✔ Remember—you are in control!

✔ Place your hands lower on the club.

SUMMARY

Incorporate your drill work on-course. Before stepping into the bunker, take several rehearsal swings outside the bunker from your key address position. You have practiced and developed your confidence with the Tee Drill and Sand Pile Drill. Feel the acceleration needed to go your desired distance. Trust your feel. Once you are comfortable with your preparation, walk into the bunker with confidence. Commit to the feel.

To lower your scores, a positive attitude is a must. Sand bunkers are everywhere on a course. You are going to be in them. Accept it, and use the tips in this chapter to conquer your fear and master the sand shot.

Lynn Marriott is one of only six women listed as *Golf Magazine*'s Top 100 Instructors. She was named the LPGA National Teacher of the Year in 1992. Marriott is actively involved with The First Tee, a golf program for disadvantaged children. She has also worked as a consultant to the LPGA Urban Youth Golf Program. She has been a consultant to many top college programs and a contributing writer for *Golf for Women Magazine*, *Golf Magazine*, *Golf Tips Magazine*, and *AZ Golf Arizona Republic*. She has been a Class A member of the LPGA since 1982 and a Class A member of the PGA since 1984.

Karrie Webb was the 1995 WPGET Rookie of the Year and the 1996 Rolex Rookie of the Year. In 1998, Karrie captured two victories and finished in the top 20 in 20 events. In 1999, she won six events, including her first major championship, and recorded 22 top-10 finishes. She claims 16 career victories.

Liselotte Neumann won the 1985 European Open, the German Open from 1986 through 1988, and the 1987 French Open. She won the 1988 U.S. Women's Open to become the 12th LPGA player to win the Open as her first tour win. Liselotte was named the 1988 LPGA Rookie of the Year. She claims 12 career victories.

6

Full-Swing Irons and Woods

Tour Professionals: Karrie Webb and Liselotte Neumann
Teaching Professional: Gale Peterson

Irons   Woods

Fortunately, the full-swing motion is not different with every club, situation, or lie. If that were the case, this would be a tough game! The fact is, you can apply the pre-swing fundamentals and iron play to the woods, and vice versa.

It is the design of the golf club that mainly governs the shot's trajectory and distance. This is why you can use the same basic full swing for most types of shots and still produce the desired flight path. You simply choose the ideal club for the shot, then execute the basic full-swing motion.

How to Hit Full-Swing Irons and Woods

SETUP

Irons are designed to approach the ball from a steeper, more descending angle, whereas woods approach it at a more sweeping, shallow angle. Irons require a slightly narrower stance than woods to allow the club to swing more vertically. Woods require a wider stance because of the longer club and sweeping angle of contact. When using irons, place the ball anywhere between the center of your stance to the point even with the target side of your face. With woods, place the ball farther toward the target, in line with your target heel.

Irons.

Woods.

SWING

Your swing motion becomes slightly more vertical as you move from the woods to the long irons to the short irons. This is created by the slightly narrower stance at address. Allow your setup to shape your swing. Remember, one swing with slight modifications in your setup.

Irons.

Woods.

How to Hit Full-Swing Irons and Woods

CONTACT

There is a gradual acceleration that begins during the forward swing and continues *through* the point of contact. It is not until the club begins to swing upward that a gradual deceleration occurs.

Irons.

Woods.

FOLLOW-THROUGH

Let your body rotation and weight shift respond to your arm swing. The swing continues until your hands are higher than your target shoulder.

Irons.

Woods.

CLUB SELECTION

The fact that there is a variety of clubs from which to choose is what allows the basic swinging motion to remain consistent for most shots. It is the design of the golf club that makes the ball fly higher, lower, shorter, or farther. Knowing some of the characteristics of the irons and woods will help you choose the ideal club for your shot.

Irons

The most common instances in which you'll choose an iron include the following:

- Starting a hole
- Trouble shots, as from under trees or over trees
- Out of high grass or divots
- Out of sand bunkers
- Par 3s
- High-lipped sand bunkers
- Approach shots

Long Irons

The long irons (1, 2, 3, 4) have the least loft and longest shaft. This combination makes them less friendly to most players. If, however, you generate a substantial amount of clubhead speed and make solid contact with a fairly high trajectory, you will be successful with these clubs. For players who create excessive sidespin, the straighter face magnifies the spin. The balls tend to fly lower and roll excessively as they hit the green. This may be a drawback if you do not hit a shot with a high trajectory. There tends to be greater variation in distance and accuracy control.

Mid-Irons

The mid-irons (5, 6, 7) are friendlier clubs than the long irons. The added loft with shorter and slightly more vertical shafts makes the mid-irons easier to swing. The swing motion creates a descending angle, which gives the ball more backspin. This allows the ball to roll less and reduces the amount of sidespin, which lessens the degree of curvature. You will be able to develop more distance and accuracy control with the mid-irons.

Short Irons

The short irons (8, 9, PW, SW, LW) are your accuracy clubs. As you get closer to the green, the importance of distance and direction control become more critical. As the number gets higher, the trajectory gets higher, and the shaft gets shorter. The clubs are heavier, shorter, and sit more vertical to the ground than the long irons, mid-irons, and woods. This combination makes for easier clubs to manage and a lot of fun hitting.

Woods

The woods can be broken down into two categories: the driver and the fairway woods.

The driver is often used for the following:

- Starting a hole
- A very good lie in the fairway (if your skill allows)
- A low-lipped fairway bunker with the ball sitting up on the sand (if your skill allows).

The fairway woods are often used for the following:

- Starting a hole
- Advancing the ball down the fairway
- High, long shots into well-guarded greens
- In place of long and/or mid-irons
- Par 3s needing height and very little roll
- Tight fairways
- Hardpan lies
- Deep rough
- Fairway bunkers

Driver

The driver is one of the most used clubs in your bag. It is used, but not required, at the start of par 4s, par 5s, and many long par 3s. It's the longest, lightest, and flattest angle to the ground with the least amount of loft. You can hit the ball the greatest distance but also the most off-line and out of play.

The expression "loft is forgiving" is very true with a driving club. There are loft options for the driving club from 6 to 12 degrees. The less-lofted drivers magnify sidespin, which sends the ball off-line and makes it difficult to get the ball to stay in the air long enough to get distance. A successful drive requires a combination of loft, length, and width in your swing, positioned clubface contact, and clubhead and ball speed, which contribute to the desired ball trajectory. The major limitation is lack of speed to produce enough backspin to get the ball airborne. Test your 3, 4, and 5 woods against your driver. Use the club that hits the ball the farthest and keeps it in play the greatest percentage of time.

Fairway Woods

The fairway woods are all other woods in your bag from the 2 wood and higher. Utility woods (5, 6, 7, 9, and 11) are quickly replacing the long and middle irons because they are so versatile; you can play them from a wide variety of lies because of the added loft, longer shaft, and design features that get the ball in the air more easily and have less roll when landing on the greens. Compared to the long irons, they are more predictable in distance and require less strength to be successful.

KARRIE WEBB'S IRON SHOT STRATEGY

Consistency is key to becoming a good golfer. I think I was fortunate to have been taught the basic fundamentals. These fundamentals are what I rely on to execute a consistent swing. I also attribute my consistency to practice and hard work. I hit a lot of greens, and even during those weeks that I'm not hitting the ball that well, I'm still on the green somewhere.

To execute a good shot, I first try to visualize the exact shot that I want to hit—from the pre-swing routine to the spot where I want the ball to land. After the shot, there's not really a lot to think about. Hopefully, I've hit a good shot, and I can begin to concentrate on the next.

When it comes to club selection and choosing, for example, between a 5 wood and a 3 iron, I think I would choose the 5 wood just because the woods these days are just so much more forgiving. I really feel that, even with a bad swing, I can get the 5 wood pretty close to the green, if not on the green. I am a fairly decent long iron player, but they are a little bit harder to hit than a 5 wood.

HITTING A GREAT 3-IRON SHOT AS A ROOKIE

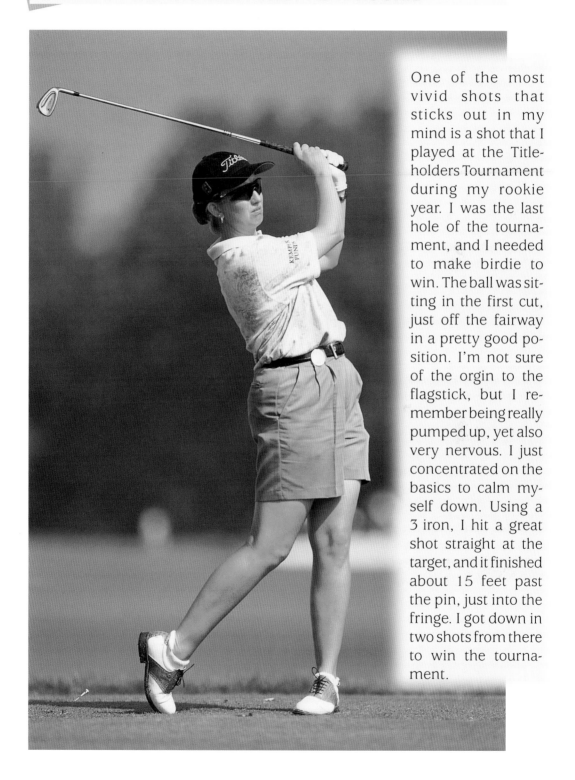

One of the most vivid shots that sticks out in my mind is a shot that I played at the Titleholders Tournament during my rookie year. I was the last hole of the tournament, and I needed to make birdie to win. The ball was sitting in the first cut, just off the fairway in a pretty good position. I'm not sure of the orgin to the flagstick, but I remember being really pumped up, yet also very nervous. I just concentrated on the basics to calm myself down. Using a 3 iron, I hit a great shot straight at the target, and it finished about 15 feet past the pin, just into the fringe. I got down in two shots from there to win the tournament.

LISELOTTE NEUMANN'S WOOD SHOT STRATEGY

First I check the lie of the ball and the wind. Then I decide how far I want to hit the ball, and I make sure to check the green to see if it is hard and will cause the ball to roll or land soft. Before the shot, I visualize the exact shot I want to hit and then take a few practice swings. Then I go behind the ball, pick a spot three to four feet in front of the ball in line with my shot. Next comes the setup and shot execution. I always have a swing thought to keep my focus.

Remember, you can only play one shot at a time. Stay within yourself. Stay focused and forget a bad shot. Think positive. Take a deep breath and relax.

In my opinion, long irons are harder to hit well, whereas woods are more forgiving and easier to hit higher. They hold the greens more than the 3 and 4 irons and are easier out of the rough.

A PERFECT 7-WOOD SHOT AT EAGLE'S LANDING

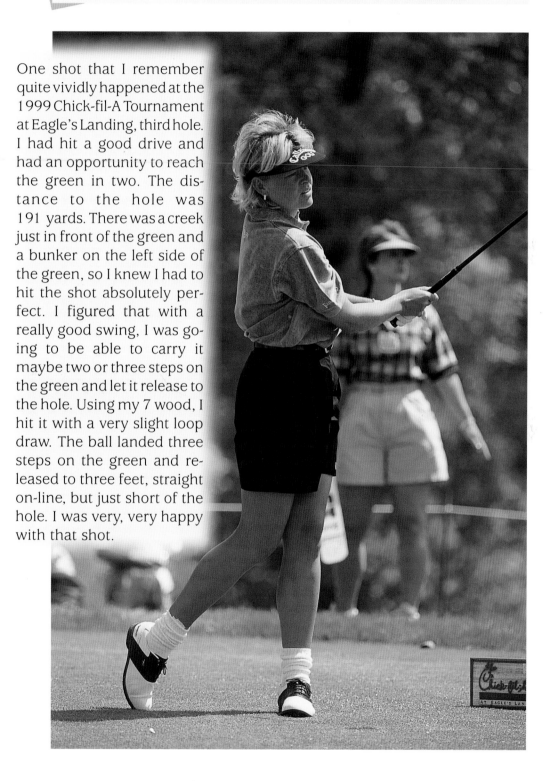

One shot that I remember quite vividly happened at the 1999 Chick-fil-A Tournament at Eagle's Landing, third hole. I had hit a good drive and had an opportunity to reach the green in two. The distance to the hole was 191 yards. There was a creek just in front of the green and a bunker on the left side of the green, so I knew I had to hit the shot absolutely perfect. I figured that with a really good swing, I was going to be able to carry it maybe two or three steps on the green and let it release to the hole. Using my 7 wood, I hit it with a very slight loop draw. The ball landed three steps on the green and released to three feet, straight on-line, but just short of the hole. I was very, very happy with that shot.

KEY DRILLS FOR IRONS

Line Drill

This drill is used to assist you in making solid contact and taking a divot on the target side of the ball. Scrape a "T" in the ground. The top of the "T" is the target line, and the other line is the ball position. Straddle the line as if the ball were on the line. Make practice swings, taking a divot from the line and forward. Repeat until you have succeeded five times.

Place a ball on the line and swing, taking a divot from the line and forward. Repeat until you have succeeded five times.

Repeat these exercises at least five times or until you can consistently take a divot.

Direction Drill

On the range select a target that is within reach of your 5 iron or 7 iron. Hit 10 shots as if you were on the golf course. Note the landing area of each shot. How consistent were your shots in direction? If the direction was inconsistent, review the section on aim and alignment in chapter 1. This is often the area that limits your ability to get direction as well as the desired distance. If you can hit 7 or more shots out of 10 in the desired direction, you are well on your way to lowering your scores.

KEY DRILLS FOR WOODS

Slope Drill

Use this drill to shallow and flatten your swing arc. This is particularly helpful if you tend to pop up your drives or hit the fairway woods fat or too steep. Find a slope with the ball above your feet. Take two practice swings, matching the swings to the slope of the hill. Address the ball. Position the ball a little forward of center for this drill, rather than inside your target heel. Hit the shot. Let the slope help to promote a shallow and inside path to the ball. Expect the ball to start more to the right if you are right-handed or to the left if you are left-handed, then expect it to curve in the direction of the downslope.

Repeat the drill five times. Then hit from a level lie. Then go back to the slope. Continue this practice until you can sweep the ball three out of five times. Your goal is to make five of five.

Three-Ball Drill

This drill will help you develop confidence in getting the ball airborne without trying to when swinging the wood. Start with your most-lofted wood. Line up three balls in a row. Place the first ball on a tee, with half the ball above the clubface and half below. Place the second ball on a tee level with the ground and the third ball on the ground. Move your hands down on the handle two to three inches. Position the ball toward your target heel. Now, swing at the first ball and clip the tee out of the ground. Swing at the second ball and clip the tee out of the ground. Swing at the third ball and clip the grass. Continue this drill until you can get the third ball in the air regularly. Then, go to the full length of the club. Repeat until you can get the third ball airborne with ease. The final step is to do the drill with no tees. Repeat the process often or as needed to be successful with your woods.

FULL-SWING SUCCESS CHECKLIST

✔ The stance for iron shots is slightly narrower than that of woods. Woods require a wider stance because of the longer club length.

✔ Adjust your posture according to the club length and distance from the ball.

✔ Position the ball center to forward of center for irons and target side of center for woods.

✔ The swing motion in the irons is more vertical in shape than that of the woods. Using the woods requires a long, wide, fluid swing.

✔ The ball positions for the driver and fairway woods are slightly different due to the lie of the ball. The driver is on a tee, and the fairway wood is on the ground. With the driver, position the ball more toward your target foot with the ball on the tee to create a sweeping to level contact with the ball. The ball position with the fairway woods is about two inches back from your target heel. The club contacts the ball slightly downward to level.

✔ Constantly assess direction and distance on the range.

✔ Select the club that gives you confidence and success.

✔ When in doubt, select the iron with more loft. Loft is forgiving.

✔ If you need a high trajectory into a green and have a choice of a long iron or utility wood, choose the wood.

SUMMARY

You can select clubs that have the potential to influence your normal flight curvature without having to change your swing. Give yourself permission to play the game with clubs that meet your needs. For example, if long irons are not your thing, try the utility woods. Even the tour professionals have chosen this route.

Practice will help you develop confidence in your directional and distance control of your irons and woods. Use your practice sessions as a measuring stick of your expectations on the course.

Gale Peterson, a PGA and LPGA member, has given private and group instruction since 1978. She has instructed PGA workshops, LPGA schools, and junior camps. She has contributed several articles to many leading golf magazines and has been a guest instructor for the Golf Channel. Gale was a featured speaker at the PGA Teaching and Coaching Summit in December 1998. She was listed as one of the 100 Greatest Teachers by *Golf Magazine* in 1996 and 1999. Gale was named the 1996 National LPGA Teacher of the Year and the 1997 Georgia PGA Teacher of the Year.

PART II

Adapting Swings
for Special Shots

Patty Sheehan was inducted into the LPGA Hall of Fame in 1993 and received the 1994 Flo Hyman award. She most recently won the 1996 Nabisco Dinah Shore, her 35th career victory and sixth major championship. Patty was one of eight athletes featured on *Sports Illustrated's* annual "Sportsman of the Year" cover in 1987.

Brandie Burton turned professional in 1991 when she qualified for the LPGA Tour on her first attempt. She was named the 1991 LPGA Rookie of the Year. *Golf World* named her the 1993 Player of the Year. In 1998, Brandie recorded her fifth career victory and second major championship at the du Maurier Classic.

7

Draws and Hooks, Fades and Slices

Tour Professionals: Patty Sheehan and Brandie Burton
Teaching Professional: Kay McMahon

Hook   Slice

As you advance in golf, you will discover the fun in adapting your basic swing fundamentals to maneuver the ball. Being able to intentionally hook or slice the ball to either avoid obstacles, such as trees, hazards, bunkers, or the like, or to position your ball in strategic spots will help you save strokes. For a right-handed player, a draw or hook is when the ball curves from right to left. A draw curves gently, and a hook, much more severely. For a right-hander, a fade or slice is when the ball curves from left to right. A fade curves gently; a slice, much more severely. Once you learn to intentionally curve the ball, you can hit target spots in fairways, create easier approaches to greens and flagsticks, and make more successful recovery shots.

How to Hit Hooks and Slices

SETUP

Aim the clubface toward your target. Align your stance and body in the initial direction you want the ball to start. Your shoulder line produces the swing path and initial direction of the ball. Align right for a hook and left for a slice. Your hand position at address and hand pressure during the swing affect the movement of your wrists through impact. This influences the clubface angle, which in turn affects the spin and resulting curvature.

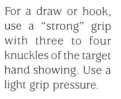

For a draw or hook, use a "strong" grip with three to four knuckles of the target hand showing. Use a light grip pressure.

For a fade or slice, use a "weak" grip with one to one and a half knuckles of the target hand showing. Use a firm grip pressure.

SWING

Make your regular swing. Alignment and swing motion control the starting direction of the ball, while the position of the clubface creates the desired hook or slice curvature.

Swing motion for the hook or draw.

Swing motion for the slice or fade.

How to Hit Hooks and Slices

CONTACT

The angle of the clubface, closed or open relative to your swing path, influences the spin or the curvature that a golf ball displays at the end of the ball flight. A closed clubface at impact results in a draw or hook. An open clubface at impact results in a fade or slice.

Use a closed clubface for the draw or hook.

Use an open clubface for the fade or slice.

FOLLOW–THROUGH

Hold the follow-through and maintain a balanced finish.

Follow-through position for the draw and hook (more release).

Follow-through position for the fade and slice (little or no release).

PATTY SHEEHAN'S HOOK STRATEGY

To execute the hook, there are a few adaptations that I make from my normal setup and swing execution. I simply overemphasize. I use a closed stance, take a strong grip, and use an inside-out swing. If conditions happen to dictate a slice, I do the opposite. I take an open stance and a weak grip and use an outside-in swing. The advantage of each shot is that you can recover from trouble from almost anywhere.

The easiest clubs to hook are the 7 iron through the 4 iron, because I can hit down on the ball and put enough spin on it to maintain the shot. The most difficult clubs to hook are the pitching wedge and 9 iron because the ball doesn't travel as far and therefore doesn't stay in the air long enough.

HITTING A HOOK SHOT AT THE SAFECO CLASSIC

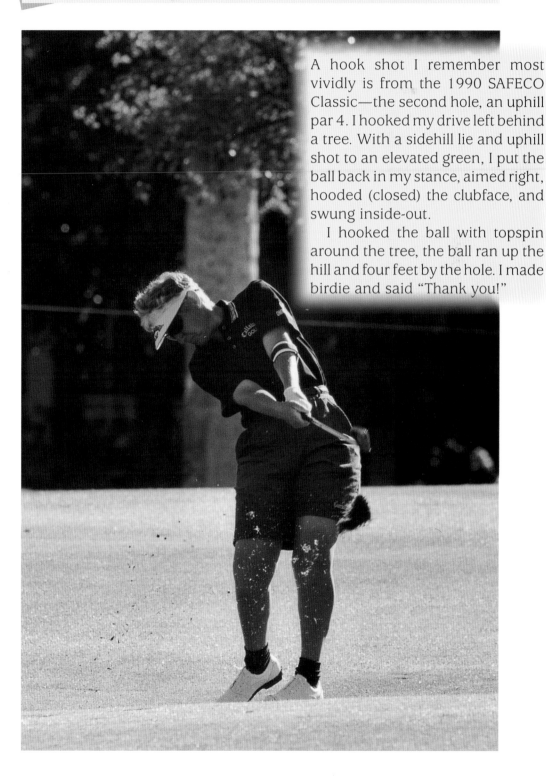

A hook shot I remember most vividly is from the 1990 SAFECO Classic—the second hole, an uphill par 4. I hooked my drive left behind a tree. With a sidehill lie and uphill shot to an elevated green, I put the ball back in my stance, aimed right, hooded (closed) the clubface, and swung inside-out.

I hooked the ball with topspin around the tree, the ball ran up the hill and four feet by the hole. I made birdie and said "Thank you!"

BRANDIE BURTON'S SLICE STRATEGY

To execute a slice, I have to change a few things in my setup. First, I open my stance, so I align my body a little left of my target. Next, I open my clubface at address to create the left-to-right spin or slice. If the conditions call for a hook, all I do is aim more right and close the clubface more than usual. Whether slicing or hooking the ball, the clubface angle at impact creates the spin to curve the ball.

Moving the ball right to left or left to right is vital during tournament play for many reasons, including getting back to the fairway from behind a tree, playing the ball away from trouble, and curving the ball to your target. There are numerous times during a round where I will maneuver the ball. I don't believe there are any disadvantages in curving the ball when you want to, other than maybe overthinking your shot.

The driver and long irons are easier to slice than the short irons. The more loft a club has, the more backspin is imparted and the less likely it will hook or slice. The driver and long irons have the least amount of loft, therefore making it easier to create more sidespin and more curve to your shot.

SLICING THE BALL AT THE 1998 DU MAURIER CLASSIC

One of my most memorable slice shots was during the 1998 du Maurier Classic, in Windsor, Ontario. It was during the third round, hole number 15. The flag position was placed in middle center. I teed off and hit it into the right rough. Trees were blocking a direct line of flight to the flag. My goal was to hit the ball 75 yards left of the flag, which led to an opening on the left side of the green. The ultimate outcome of the shot was approximately 15 feet left of the hole, pin high.

This shot was one of the most important shots I had to execute during this tournament. The confidence and momentum it gave me led to my most recent win and, ultimately, my second win of the du Maurier Classic.

KEY DRILLS FOR HOOKS AND SLICES

Hand Position Drill

Hit a ball with your standard hand position and mark where the ball lands. Rotate your hand so you can see one knuckle of your target hand, then hit the ball again. Evaluate the flight and note where the ball lands in relation to the first ball. Rotate the position of your hand again so you can see one and a half knuckles on your target hand, then repeat the drill. Continue to repeat the drill as you rotate your grip so you can see two, three, and four knuckles of your target hand. Note how your ball flies with each grip and evaluate how you can use each to intentionally curve the ball to a specific target.

Hand Pressure Drill

Experiment with different hand pressures. Place your hands on the club with your regular pressure and hit a ball. Observe the ball flight and notice where the ball lands. Now hold the club lighter and hit another shot, once again evaluating the ball flight and spotting where the ball lands. Finally, hold on tighter than normal and hit a shot, observing the ball flight and noticing the direction the ball travels. Light hand pressure will encourage hand and wrist action and close the clubface at contact, resulting in draw-to-hook curvature. A tighter grip pressure will reduce hand action and open the clubface at contact, resulting in a fade-to-slice curvature.

Slice Alignment Drill

Pick a target. Using a 5 iron, aim your clubface at the target. Next align your body 20 degrees left of your intended target to where you intend the ball's initial direction to be. Hit five balls. Observe and experience the results. Now align your body 40 degrees left of your intended target, clubface at the target, and hit five shots. Observe the resulting curvature. Finally, align your body 50 degrees left of your target, clubface still aimed at your target, and hit five more shots, observing the resulting ball flight. Which produces a gentle fade and which produces a severe slice? See if you can work your ball back to your intended target.

Hook Alignment Drill

Pick a target. Using a 5 iron, aim your clubface at the target. Next align your body 20 degrees right of your intended target to where you intend the ball's initial direction to be. Hit five balls. Observe and experience the results. Now align your body 40 degrees right of your intended target, clubface at the target, and hit five shots. Observe the resulting curvature. Finally, align your body 50 degrees right of your target, clubface still aimed at your target, and hit five more shots, observing the resulting ball flight. Which position produces a gentle draw and which produces a severe hook? See if you can work your ball back to your intended target.

Shoulder Path Drill

Using a 5 iron, stand square to your target and experiment by changing your shoulder path through impact while using various hand or wrist manipulations to spin the ball to the right and left. Start by attempting to have your shoulders point right of your intended target, and using your wrists, manipulate the clubface closed to produce a shot that starts right of your target and hooks back toward it. Attempt this with five shots. Now try to make your shoulders point to the left of your target at contact, and manipulate your wrists to open the clubface and produce a fade or slice that starts left of your target and curves back toward it. Play a game, calling your shots before execution.

Obstacle Drill

Find trees and attempt to curve your ball around them. Move closer and farther away from the tree. Use different clubs, a 5 iron, 7 iron, and 3 wood, and see which club you have more success with. Generally clubs with less loft are easier to make curve because less backspin is imparted with less loft, providing for more sidespin. Visualize the shot. Apply the principles, then trust that you can curve the ball.

Visualize-and-Swing Drill

On the range, imagine you are on the golf course and visualize situations that require you to fade, slice, draw, and hook a shot. For example, a dog-leg left where a draw from the tee will result in extra yardage. Use your driver and the method you have found to be most successful for your attempt to hit the shot you visualize. The next shot may be a softly fading 7 iron to access an imagined front pin placement on a firm green.

HOOK AND SLICE SUCCESS CHECKLIST

✔ Generally the less-lofted clubs are the easier to intentionally curve, because less backspin is imparted to the ball and more sidespin is created.

✔ A hand position with three to four knuckles of the target hand showing, along with a light grip pressure, will enhance the movement of your wrists and close the clubface to create the draw-to-hook curvature. In a firm grip with one to one and a half knuckles of the target hand showing, your hand action will be reduced in your swing, helping to create an open clubface at impact and a fade-to-slice curvature.

✔ Shoulder direction at contact influences the path of the clubhead, which in turn affects the initial direction of the ball.

✔ These are the times you'll most likely want to hit an intentional hook:

   Dog-leg right-to-left

   Pin position on left edge of green

   Bunker guarding left side of green

   Ball behind a tree or other obstacle

   Extra distance and roll needed

✔ These are the times you'll most likely want to hit an intentional slice:

   Dog-leg left-to-right

   Pin position on right edge of green

   Bunker guarding right side of green

   Ball behind a tree or other obstacle

   When the greens are firm and you need the ball to land softly

SUMMARY

Learning to work the ball introduces creativity and fun into your game. Remember to aim your clubface where you want the ball to finish and align your body where you want the ball to initially begin. Then trust yourself and swing along your body lines. Being creative, using your imagination, and knowing how to make your ball intentionally curve may produce lower scores and generate the fun of the game. Enjoy . . . call your shot.

Kay McMahon is the head instructor at the Mission Hills Country Club Learning Center in Palm Springs, California. She is a Class A Member of both the LPGA and the PGA. She was the national president of the LPGA Teaching and Club Professional Division from 1998 to 1999 and currently writes as a teaching panelist for *Golf Digest.* Kay was honored as the 1995 National LPGA Teacher of the Year and received four awards as the Western Section Teacher of the Year. She is also president and CEO of Kayline Sports Consulting, Inc.

Juli Inkster became the first person to win three consecutive U.S. Amateur titles in 1982 and became the first rookie to win two major championships in one season in 1984. In 1999, she missed only one cut in 24 starts and posted 18 top-10 finishes, including all four majors. Juli earned her way into the LPGA Hall of Fame by capturing five tournaments, including two majors, for a career total 22.

8

Uneven Lies

Tour Professional: Juli Inkster
Teaching Professional: Dana Rader

Downhill lie   Uphill lie

The game of golf would be simpler if we could play on level land. It is all the twists and turns, slopes in the course, the dreaded downhill lies, and uphill and sidehill shots that really make golf a game of science as well as one of skill. Understanding what changes to make in your setup and swing and what ball flight each uneven lie is likely to produce is a part of that science—and the fun in golf. When you understand how to play off uneven lies, you'll be able to visualize the ball flight and score more effectively.

How to Hit Downhill Lies

SETUP

Your weight should be on your target side, and your shoulders should match the slope. Position the ball more toward your high foot. The more severe the slope, the farther back you should play the ball. Aim your clubface and align your body to the left of the target to allow the shot to react to the slope and to compensate for its normal tendency to be low and fade to the right.

SWING

Keep your body quiet and allow your arms to swing down the slope. The slope will deloft your club and produce a low trajectory, so make sure you've selected a club with more loft. If you would normally use a 5 wood, use a 7 wood to get the required loft. Longer clubs, such as a 3 wood, are difficult to hit off downhill lies due to their length and small amount of loft.

How to Hit Uphill Lies

SETUP

Your weight should be on your rear foot and your shoulders should be parallel to the slope. Your ball position should be slightly more forward than usual or toward your high foot. The more severe the slope, the more forward you should position the ball.

SWING

You should take one or two more clubs than normal because the slope effectively adds loft to your club and shots. The more severe the slope, the more club you need to use. The less you move your feet, especially your rear foot, the more your club can swing toward your target.

How to Hit Sidehill Lies—Ball Below Feet

SETUP

Align your body to the left of the target. Position your weight more toward your toes, with the slope. Balance is the key. Position the ball in the center of your stance.

SWING

Swing with a quiet body. You will feel like you are swinging more with your arms and with less footwork and body movement than from a flat lie. Trust your swing and allow your alignment and the slope to carry the ball to your target.

How to Hit Sidehill Lies—Ball Above Feet

SETUP

Aim to the right of your target. The more severe the slope and the greater the loft of the club, the more you must aim to the right. Your weight again goes with the slope, balanced toward your heels. Position the ball in the center of your stance.

SWING

Keep your body and feet quiet, and allow your arms to swing along the slope and carry your ball to your target.

JULI INKSTER'S UNEVEN LIES STRATEGY

When it comes to hitting from uneven lies, I just follow the contour of the hill and let the ball flight take its course. I also move my hands down on the club and try to take more of a three-quarter swing than a full swing. That way I hit the ball a little crisper.

I use a lower-number club on a sidehill lie when the ball is below my feet in an effort to make up for the distance I'll lose because of the lie. In a sidehill lie, the ball will not go straight, so you really have to work the ball, and strategy-wise, you must locate and avoid any obstacles. For example, if I had a shot where my feet were above the ball and water was to the right, naturally I would aim more left to avoid the water. The bottom line is to make sure you hit the fairway and swing in balance.

When it comes to club choice, I think the 8s, 7s, and 6s are the easiest because they are shorter irons. I think the hardest ones are definitely the longer clubs, because you're liable to stub the ground before you hit the ball. You really have to maintain your balance and the levelness of your swing.

A TOURNAMENT-WINNING SIDEHILL SHOT

One very memorable shot took place at a tournament in Sacramento on the 17th hole. I had a sidehill lie with my feet below the ball. It was on a par 5. I started to move my hands down on a 3 wood just to get the ball rolling in the right direction. With a sidehill lie in which my feet are below the ball, I always aim a little more right, because naturally the ball is going to go right to left. Instead of trying to change my swing to get the ball to go straight, I just follow the contour of the hill. In this case, I hit it right down the middle, made par on the hole, and won the tournament.

KEY DRILLS FOR UNEVEN LIES

Downhill Lie Drill

Find a downhill lie. Sometimes the sides of practice facilities have mounds that provide excellent uneven lies. Use a 7 iron. Make the necessary compensations for the lie by moving the ball more toward your back foot, matching your torso to the slope, and aiming slightly left of your target. Take a few practice swings and notice where your club contacts the ground. Hit three balls, observing the ball flights. How does your ball flight compare to your normal 7-iron trajectory from a flat lie? Is the ball flight lower? Does the ball tend to curve to the right? Does the ball travel farther or shorter than normal? Repeat this exercise using a 5 iron, 7 wood, and 3 wood. If possible, repeat this exercise from both a more severe downhill lie and a less severe downhill lie and observe the resulting ball flights.

Uphill Lie Drill

Find an uphill lie. Make the necessary compensations for an uphill lie by moving the ball forward in your stance, matching your torso to the slope, and aiming slightly right of your intended target. Using a 7 iron, take a few practice swings. Hit three balls with your 7 iron. How does the ball flight compare to your normal 7-iron trajectory from a flat lie? Is the ball flight higher? Does the ball tend to curve to the left? Does the ball carry shorter than normal? Repeat this exercise using a 5 iron, 7 wood, and 3 wood. If possible, repeat this exercise from both a more severe uphill lie and a less severe uphill lie and observe the resulting ball flights.

Uneven Lie Drill (Ball Below Feet)

Find an uneven lie where the ball is below your feet. Make the necessary compensations for this sidehill lie by aiming left of your intended target, positioning your weight more toward your toes, and centering the ball in your stance. Swing with quiet feet so you can maintain your balance. Using a 7 iron, take a few practice swings. Hit three balls with your 7 iron. How does the ball flight compare to your normal 7-iron trajectory from a flat lie? Is the ball flight lower? Does the ball tend to curve to the right? Does the ball carry shorter than normal? Repeat this exercise using a 5 iron, 7 wood, and 3 wood. If possible, repeat this exercise from both a more severe uneven lie where the ball is more below your feet and a less severe sidehill lie where the ball is not as far below your feet and observe the resulting ball flights.

Uneven Lie Drill (Ball Above Feet)

Find an uneven lie where the ball is above your feet. Make the necessary compensations for this sidehill lie by aiming right of your intended target, positioning your weight more toward your heels, and centering the ball in your stance. Swing with quiet feet so you can maintain your balance. Using a 7 iron, take a few practice swings. Hit three balls with your 7 iron. How does the ball flight compare to your normal 7-iron trajectory from a flat lie? Is the ball flight lower or higher? Does the ball tend to curve to the left? Does the ball carry shorter or farther than normal? Repeat this exercise using a 5 iron, 7 wood, and 3 wood. Notice which club tends to be more affected by the sidehill lie. Is it the more-lofted club or the less-lofted club? If possible repeat this exercise using the same four clubs, from a more severe uneven lie where the ball is more above your feet and a less severe sidehill lie where the ball is not as far above your feet and observe the resulting ball flights.

If you have the opportunity, hit some of these shots out on the course during quiet times. Be observant of the slope's effect so that in an actual round you will be able to visualize the probable ball flight and make the necessary compensations.

UNEVEN LIES SUCCESS CHECKLIST

✔ Understand what club to use and the effect the various uneven lies have on the loft.

✔ Uneven sidehill lies affect the more-lofted clubs more than less-lofted clubs.

✔ The more severe the slope, the greater the effect and the more you must compensate.

✔ Understand what compensations you must make in your setup for the various sidehill lies.

✔ Match your torso to the slope.

✔ Swing in balance.

✔ Visualize the shot and the effect the slope is going to have, then allow the slope to work for you.

SUMMARY

To be successful when you are playing from uneven lies, you need to consider the club you are using and the severity of the slope. The greater the club's loft, the greater the effect will be on the ball. It is usually best to take more club, for example, a 5 iron versus a 6 iron, and swing with slightly less speed because you will have better balance. Also, the ball will not spin as much because you chose the less-lofted club.

The key to uneven lies is understanding what compensations you need to make and allowing the slope's effect on the ball flight work for you. Remember, balance is of utmost importance. Recognizing where to place the ball in your stance, where your weight should be positioned, what club is required, and how the ball will react to different slopes is essential for success. The more severe the slope, the more it will affect the ball flight. The more-lofted the club, the more the slope will affect the shot, particularly on sidehill lies. Be creative, swing in balance, and allow the slopes to work for you!

Dana Rader turned professional in 1980 and was honored in 1990 as the LPGA's National Teacher of the Year. In 1996 and 1999, she was named one of the Top 100 Teachers in the United States by *Golf Magazine.* She received the Top 25 Women in Business Achievement award by *The Business Journal* in 1998. Dana has written for many leading publications, appears regularly on the Golf Channel, and serves on the advisory board for Nancy Lopez Golf. She is the Director of Golf at Ballantyne Resort's Golf Club in Charlotte, North Carolina.

Kelly Robbins was a member of the University of Tulsa's 1988 NCAA Championship team and named the 1991 NCAA Co-Player of the Year. She claimed one LPGA major championship and nine other top-10 finishes in 1995. Kelly recorded her ninth career victory in 1999 at the HEALTHSOUTH Inaugural where she tied her career-low round of 64 during the final round.

Tammie Green was named the 1987 LPGA Rookie of the Year, had five top-10 finishes in 1988, and became a Rolex First-Time Winner by capturing the 1989 du Maurier Classic. She was named 1989's Most Improved Player by *Golf Digest*. Tammie has seven career victories.

9

High and Low Shots

Tour Professionals: Kelly Robbins and Tammie Green
Teaching Professional: Sharon Miller

High shot   Low shot

As your swing becomes more consistent and your scores improve, you will need to learn to hit the ball intentionally high and low in order to save shots during your round. You can use high trajectory shots to cut dog-legs, hold greens, take advantage of tailwinds, and recover from wayward tee shots. You can use low trajectory shots in windy conditions, to run the ball onto the greens, to access back pin positions, or on recovery shots under trees or low branches.

Altering your ball flight is relatively easy. You can use your normal swing motion with only subtle changes in your setup. The height of your shot is determined by the angle of approach and the amount of loft on the clubface as the club contacts the ball. For the ball to get airborne, you must contact it below its equator. A ball contacted above its equator results in a topped, or thin, shot. For a higher shot, you must increase the normal loft of your clubface at contact, and for a lower shot, you must reduce the amount of loft at contact.

How to Hit High and Low Shots

SETUP

For a high shot, place the ball more forward (one to two ball-widths) in your stance than a regular shot. For a low shot, place the ball farther back (one to three ball-widths) than normal. In a high shot, your hands need to be even or a little behind the ball, whereas in a low shot your hands need to be positioned farther ahead of the ball than normal because of the ball's position. Your stance in a high shot is square or slightly open to promote a more upright swing. In a low shot, use a square or slightly closed stance to promote a flatter swing plane.

For a high shot, position the ball more forward in your stance.

For a low shot, position the ball farther back in your stance.

SWING

In a high shot, your weight should slightly favor your rear side throughout the swing (60 percent rear side, 40 percent target side). In a low shot, it's just the opposite (60 percent target side, 40 percent rear side). The high shot calls for a lighter grip to promote a fuller, "wristier" backswing. In the low shot, use a firmer grip to eliminate any wrist hinge and to keep your hands firm through the hitting area. This helps keep the clubhead moving along the target line longer.

The high shot calls for a fuller, "wristier" backswing.

Avoid hinging your wrists in the low shot.

How to Hit High and Low Shots

CONTACT

The high shot uses more wrists and hands in the swing, especially at the bottom of the swing. This looser, "flippier" hand action where the rear hand "works under," or·stays more under the shaft, will result in your rear hand being slightly ahead of the target hand at contact, increasing the effective loft of the club. In the low shot, take a shorter, more compact swing to minimize wrist action.

The high shot requires more hand and wrist action at the bottom of the swing.

The low shot requires a shorter, more compact swing.

FOLLOW-THROUGH

Finish with your hands high to hit it high. Follow through low to hit it low. In a low shot, your hands should finish about waist-high with the clubhead pointing toward the target.

A high shot demands a high follow-through.

A low shot demands a low follow-through.

KELLY ROBBINS'S HIGH SHOT STRATEGY

In preparing for a shot, I try to keep things fairly simple. I picture the perfect shot and what I want the ball to do. I also work on a good setup and ball positioning and try to prepare myself as well as I can physically before I hit the shot. I just try to go through the routine and hit the shot how I always do.

To hit high shots, I have to slightly adjust my normal routine by playing the ball a little more forward in my stance and possibly opening the clubface a little bit. It depends on what club I have and how high I have to hit it. Of course, I also have to move the ball into position, which for a high shot means moving it more forward in my stance.

I think the easiest clubs to use for high shots are the more-lofted clubs like the 8s, 9s, and wedges. It's always harder to hit a less-lofted club higher.

ESCAPING TROUBLE WITH THE HIGH SHOT

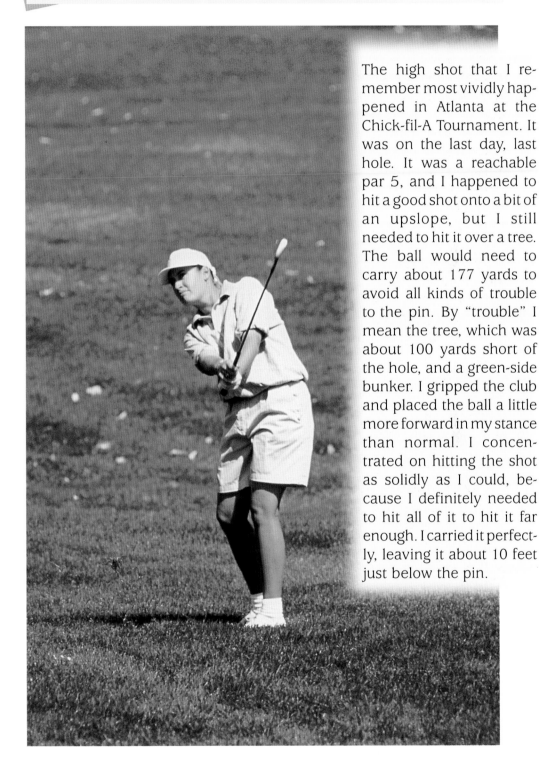

The high shot that I remember most vividly happened in Atlanta at the Chick-fil-A Tournament. It was on the last day, last hole. It was a reachable par 5, and I happened to hit a good shot onto a bit of an upslope, but I still needed to hit it over a tree. The ball would need to carry about 177 yards to avoid all kinds of trouble to the pin. By "trouble" I mean the tree, which was about 100 yards short of the hole, and a green-side bunker. I gripped the club and placed the ball a little more forward in my stance than normal. I concentrated on hitting the shot as solidly as I could, because I definitely needed to hit all of it to hit it far enough. I carried it perfectly, leaving it about 10 feet just below the pin.

TAMMIE GREEN'S LOW SHOT STRATEGY

I will hit exclusively low shots if the conditions dictate, such as a very windy day. I also use low shots when I am faced with a trouble shot where a low trajectory will allow the best opportunity for recovery. I practice low shots with most of my clubs, but have the most success controlling trajectory with my longer irons. When practicing, I try to visualize the different conditions and alter my ball flight. I can rely on this shot, but only because I have years of practice.

To hit a low shot, I make sure my hands are a little forward and that the ball is farther back in my stance. I sometimes go down on the shaft. My backswing may be a little more abrupt and my legs will drive down and forward through the hitting area, which in turn will produce a shorter follow-through.

The low shot is one I will use late in the round if I absolutely have to hit the green, because for me it is a very controlled shot. Under pressure it allows me to swing harder than normal and still control the distance, thus taking some of the anxiety out of the moment. The low shot is one of my favorite shots, and I have confidence in its execution.

HITTING A LOW SHOT AT THE CORNING CLASSIC

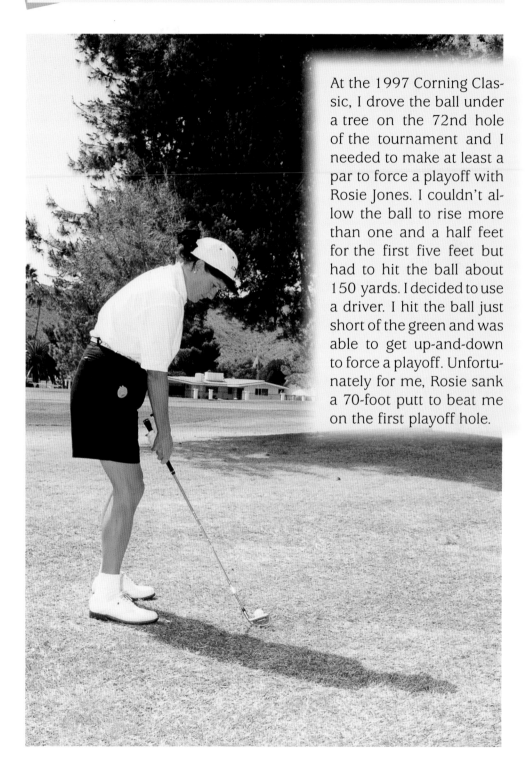

At the 1997 Corning Classic, I drove the ball under a tree on the 72nd hole of the tournament and I needed to make at least a par to force a playoff with Rosie Jones. I couldn't allow the ball to rise more than one and a half feet for the first five feet but had to hit the ball about 150 yards. I decided to use a driver. I hit the ball just short of the green and was able to get up-and-down to force a playoff. Unfortunately for me, Rosie sank a 70-foot putt to beat me on the first playoff hole.

KEY DRILLS FOR HIGH AND LOW SHOTS

Cross-Legged Drill

This exercise will teach you the importance of accelerating your arms on the downswing to hit a high shot. If you are a right-handed golfer, cross your right leg over your left leg. Hit some shots. Making your legs inactive and encouraging your arms to swing will help to promote a U-shaped, bottom-of-the-arc swing, which produces the angle of approach necessary for a high shot. (If you have back problems, avoid this drill.)

Ball Placement Drill

Using a 7 iron, hit three shots with your normal trajectory. Notice your ball position. Now move the ball one ball-width forward in your stance, and hit three shots. Notice the change in trajectory. Next move the ball one more ball-width forward, and hit three shots. Again, observe the ball's trajectory. Do the same thing, only with the ball farther back in your stance. Start with one ball-width back from your normal position, hit three shots, and observe the trajectory. Finally, move the ball back two ball-widths from its normal position, hit three shots, and note the ball's trajectory.

Club-Swapping Drill

Start with a pitching wedge. Hit a shot with normal trajectory, and then change your ball position and hit a higher shot, then a lower shot. Now switch to an 8 iron and repeat. Use every even-numbered club in your bag. Your next practice session, use every odd-numbered club, hitting a normal trajectory shot, followed by a higher trajectory shot, and then a lower shot.

Visualize-and-Swing Drill

On the practice range, create imaginary obstacles and visualize shots that go under and over the obstacle. Call your shot before you execute it.

Obstacle Drill

If possible, practice hitting shots over and under trees at the edge of the practice facility or at quiet times on your golf course.

One-Against-One Drill

Compete with another golfer, playing high-low shot games with points going to the golfer with the successful shots.

HIGH AND LOW SHOT SUCCESS CHECKLIST

✔ Visualize the shot you want to hit, whether it is over a tree or under the tree's limbs.

✔ For a high shot, move the ball forward in your stance, move your weight more toward your rear foot, and finish high.

✔ For a low shot, move the ball back in your stance, move your weight more over your forward foot, and finish low.

✔ You can alter the effective loft of any club, but generally a more-lofted club is easier to hit higher, and a less-lofted club is easier to hit lower.

SUMMARY

The trajectory of your shots is influenced by the clubhead's angle of approach at contact. Your ball position and where your club contacts the ball influence your trajectory. Understanding how to control the trajectory of your golf ball can help you go over and under trees and get your ball back in play from places you previously would have had to chip sideways. A high trajectory will give you the ability to stay on firm greens and access pins cut just over bunkers or on edges of greens as well as take advantage of downwind shots where added yardage is beneficial. Low shots will enable you to play more successfully in windy conditions. Being able to control trajectory will add to your shot selection and help you shoot lower scores. Understand what makes the ball go high and low: experiment on the practice range—then trust yourself on the course.

Sharon Miller has made her career in golf since 1966 when she joined the LPGA Tour. She won three tournaments before she retired in 1981. Sharon joined the LPGA Teaching Division, helped start *Golf for Women* magazine, and wrote as the teaching editor in chief until 1994. In 1989, she received the LPGA National Teacher of the Year award. Sharon has remained active in tournament competition and won the 1985 National Teaching Division Championship, the 1986 Women's Colorado Open, and is a three-time winner with partner Kathy Farrer in the Square Two LPGA T&CP Division team championship.

Beth Daniel won the U.S. Women's Amateur in 1975 and 1977 and was a member of the World Cup team in 1978. She was named the 1979 LPGA Rookie of the Year. In 1994, Beth won her third Rolex Player of the Year award and her third Vare Trophy honor. She owns 32 career victories including one major.

10

Fairway Bunkers

Tour Professional: Beth Daniel
Teaching Professional: Jane Frost

You've hit a beautiful drive down the left center of the fairway only to catch the downslope, which escorts your ball into the gaping mouth of a fairway bunker. The LPGA Tour professionals approach these shots confidently because they know what conditions to consider and what adjustments to make. You are going to hit the occasional drive into a fairway bunker. This chapter will help you understand how to extricate your ball from a fairway bunker with confidence and ease.

How to Hit Out of Fairway Bunkers

SETUP

The setup position for a fairway bunker shot is quite similar to that of the regular full swing. Stabilize your feet in the sand by digging in slightly with the balls of your feet. Move your hands down one to two inches on the club. Your weight distribution should favor your target side, and the ball position should be slightly farther back in your stance than normal.

Because your feet are slightly dug into the ground, you need to compensate by moving your hands down one to two inches on the club.

SWING

Once you have chosen a club with plenty of loft, stabilized your feet, gripped down on the club, and completed your setup, then the time has come to simply swing. Swing with confidence!

You want your feet to be stable and balanced, but not embedded like you would for a green-side bunker shot.

How to Hit Out of Fairway Bunkers

CONTACT

Unlike green-side bunkers, you want to contact the bottom of the ball—not the sand before the ball.

This is just like a fairway shot with an iron—ball first and then grass or sand.

FOLLOW-THROUGH

Look at your target and trust your swing. Then watch the ball soaring—right where you want it to go. Maintain good balance as you finish.

Play the ball out of the bunker, and enjoy your next shot from the short green grass.

BETH DANIEL'S FAIRWAY BUNKER STRATEGY

Fairway bunker shots are any shots that from a bunker would require you to contact the ball prior to the sand in order to achieve the desired distance. Obviously this shot is used from bunkers, but it is also beneficial when playing from sandy, rocky desert conditions and can be used from waste bunkers. Waste bunkers are dirt or sand areas that are not marked as hazards, where you are permitted to ground your club and take practice swings.

AP Photo/Peter Cosgrove

I am faced with a fairway bunker shot an average of two or three times during a tournament, sometimes more often on heavily bunkered courses. I let the lie of the ball, the distance from the lip, and the height of the lip dictate my strategy. This information also influences my club selection. I always choose a club that will safely get over the lip of the bunker. Sometimes this is a 3 wood, and sometimes all I can do is use my sand wedge and get the ball back in play.

In approaching a fairway bunker shot, I get my yardage and then select one-half to one club more, depending on the texture of the sand. If the sand is firm, I select one-half club more, and in soft sand, I use one club more. Rarely do you get a perfect lie, so I always make sure to take the club that will get me over the lip and out of the bunker.

I enjoy practicing this shot, because it is a great way to determine how crisply you are making contact. Your swing path must be good to execute this shot well. I set my feet in the sand so that the weight is on the insides of both feet. This keeps me stable throughout the shot. I also move my hands down slightly on the grip to compensate for my feet digging into the sand. I use a more controlled swing, and that is why I take a little more club.

A WINNING FAIRWAY BUNKER SHOT

The fairway bunker shot I remember most vividly was at a minitour event before I qualified for the LPGA Tour. It was on a par 5, on a windy day. I hit my second shot into a fairway bunker, and I had about 95 yards to the pin. I decided to use a pitching wedge, because it's a good idea to play about a half a club longer than what you would play out of the fairway. I choked down on it a little bit and hit a very good shot. It landed past the pin, spun back into the hole for eagle, and I won the minitour event by one shot because of it.

KEY DRILLS FOR FAIRWAY BUNKER SHOTS

Contact Drill

It is often difficult to find a fairway bunker to practice from, but sand at a beach or playground will work. Simply having some sand to rehearse from is extremely valuable even if the surroundings won't allow for the hitting of golf balls. Perhaps you could use Wiffle balls or pine cones. It's the sand more so than the ball that you need to be practicing in so that confidence rules during your next sand encounter. Once you have found some sand, use a small object or your imagination and swing, doing your best to contact the sand after the imaginary ball. If you can contact the sand where you want, you will be successful from the fairway bunkers.

Divot Drill

Draw a circle in the sand to represent the ball. Take a swing, and after the swing look at the sand and where the club made a divot. If there is no divot, chances are you topped the ball. If the divot is behind the ball, then you probably hit the shot fat. Experiment until your divot is exactly where you want it to be—in front of the ball.

Lip Distance Drill

If you have a fairway bunker from which to practice, hit shots from different distances from the lip. Start three feet from the lip. Using a wedge, hit three shots, and notice how many were a success. Now use a 7 iron from the same position, and hit another three balls. Did they all clear the lip? Next use a 5 iron from the same position, and rate your success. Finally attempt this fairway bunker shot with your 5 wood. Did the balls carry over the lip? Move back three more feet, and repeat this exercise. Finally move back another three feet, so you are nine feet from the lip, and repeat this exercise. Depending on the distance from the lip, you may need to use a sand wedge blast or perhaps you can use a fairway wood. Experiment. Practice fairway bunker shots with a variety of clubs.

Assorted Lies Drill

Practice fairway bunker shots from different lies. Instead of giving yourself a perfect lie, gently toss the ball in the bunker and play the ball where it comes to rest. Start well back from the lip (10 to 15 feet). Hit three balls with your wedge. The first ball should be a perfect lie, the second ball a worse lie, and the third ball a half-buried, bad lie. Repeat this exercise with your 7 iron, 5 iron, and 5 wood. Learn what clubs you can use from the various lies you are likely to encounter. Depending on the lie, you may need to blast your ball back into the fairway with a sand wedge or perhaps you can be successful with a 3 wood.

Varying the Lie and Distance Drill

Once you have tried the other exercises and have an idea what club is successful from the various lies and from the various distances from the lip, combine the two. Start 3 feet from the lip with a perfect lie, a poorer lie, and a nasty, half-buried lie, then use your judgment to select a club you think you can extricate the ball with. Move back another 3 feet, and repeat the exercise. Finally, back up to 9 to 10 feet from the lip, and repeat the exercise once more.

FAIRWAY BUNKER SUCCESS CHECKLIST

✔ Choose a club with enough loft to clear the lip. Err on the side of too much loft.

✔ Choose a club with enough loft to extricate your ball from your given lie.

✔ Dig your feet in slightly.

✔ Move hands down one to two inches on the grip.

✔ Position the ball slightly farther back in your stance.

✔ Contact the ball before the sand.

✔ Swing with confidence.

SUMMARY

The lie of the ball is going to determine your options in a fairway bunker. If you have a poor or buried lie or your ball is close to the lip, play a safe shot to get your ball back on the short grass. If the ball has a good lie, consider the amount of lip and the ball's distance from it, then select a club with enough loft to easily clear the lip. Make the necessary adjustments in your setup, then swing with confidence. There is no such thing as failure, only opportunities to learn. Practice builds competence, and competence builds confidence. You are now destined to succeed.

Jane Frost, a class A LPGA and PGA professional, is the head professional and director of instruction at Holly Ridge Golf Club. She was the 1994 LPGA National Teacher of the Year and the 1996 New England PGA Teacher of the Year. She has also been named the 1998 PGA Cape Cod Chapter Teacher of the Year. Jane was listed as one of *Golf Magazine*'s Top 100 Teachers in America. She is a past president and three-time tournament champion of the LPGA Teaching and Club Professional Division's Northeast Section. Jane is currently an instructor for the LPGA's National Education Program Series and is a member of the advisory board for Nancy Lopez Golf.

Michelle McGann became a three-time Florida State Junior champion and was ranked number one in 1987 by *Golf Magazine* and *Golf Digest* before she joined the tour in 1988 at the age of 18. In 1995, Michelle claimed her first of seven career victories at the Sara Lee Classic. She is the founder of the Michelle McGann Golf Classic to benefit the Diabetes Research Institute.

11

Fairway Rough

Tour Professional: Michelle McGann
Teaching Professional: Jane Frost

The fairway rough can create anguish even for the most experienced LPGA Tour professionals. Just four inches off the fairway can spell disaster if the player isn't smart about the choices that are at hand. Often, players are so angry about the rough lie that all reason is absent and false bravado and expectations take over.

The deeper the rough, the more difficult the ball will be to get out. Club selection is crucial to a successful shot from the rough. The long, thick blades of grass are going to act like giant fingers grabbing at the neck of the clubhead, strangling its forward progress toward the ball. As this happens, the clubface is twisted off-line to the left, and the loft is decreased. For example, in severe rough, a 5 iron will act more like a 2 iron as the grass envelopes the neck and clubhead. In severe rough, a highly lofted club is the best choice for advancing the ball back to the fairway. Be smart, swallow your pride, and get back in play.

How to Hit Out of Fairway Rough

SETUP

Because the grass will wrap around the neck of the club and twist the clubface off-line to the left, your aim at address should be to the right of where you want the ball to end up.

Open the clubface and your stance slightly.

SWING

Relax and hold the club slightly firmer than normal throughout the swing. This will provide extra stability and help keep the clubface square as the club travels through the rough.

Hinge your wrists early on your backswing.

How to Hit Out of Fairway Rough

CONTACT

You will have more success getting the clubface on the ball with a steep angle of approach. By using a lofted club, opening the clubface slightly, and hinging your wrists early on your backswing, you'll create a steep arc that returns the clubhead back to the ball at an angle that allows for better contact with the ball.

The more buried the ball is in the rough, the more challenging it will be to get the clubface cleanly on the ball.

FOLLOW-THROUGH

As the grass wraps around the neck of the club, clubhead speed is drastically diminished. In fact, following through may not be feasible. Take several practice swings in the rough to see what sort of grabbing is going to happen. You may require more club than you would from the same distance in the fairway.

The follow-through is not important; getting the clubface as cleanly as possible on the ball is the objective for those deeply buried rough lies.

MICHELLE MCGANN'S FAIRWAY ROUGH STRATEGY

Anytime your ball is off the fairway and the grass is going to wrap around your club, you need to use the fairway rough technique to escape the grass. At some golf courses you won't encounter any rough, while at others it will be severe. The length of grass determines much of the rough's severity, but so does the type of grass. Bermuda grass can be quite short but extremely wiry and coarse.

When you find your ball in the rough, you must use smart course management. You need to assess the lie of the ball, the length and thickness of the rough, and the direction the grass is growing. If you are going with the grass, then the ball will fly much farther. If you're hitting against the grass, the grass will grab the club. You'll have to open the clubface up a little bit so when the club comes into the heavy rough, it squares it up.

You must also honestly assess your own physical strengths and limitations. Lies that some players can advance their ball from may be lies from which others should pitch the ball back to the fairway. What is the safest way to get your ball back in a good position to play from? In the most severe cases, this may mean taking an unplayable lie. It will cost you one stroke but may save you many more in the long run. Often from severe rough your only option will be to take a sand wedge or pitching wedge and hit the ball a short distance back onto the fairway. When you do believe you have the ability and the lie permits you to attempt to advance the ball toward the green, remember to use one more club, because the rough will slow the club down. Utility woods, such as 7 and 9 woods, have enabled many players who could not hit a 3 or 4 iron from the rough to get more distance and a better trajectory from the rough. Perhaps adding one of these clubs to your bag is a necessity if you play a course with thick rough.

A MEMORABLE FAIRWAY ROUGH SHOT

A fairway rough shot during tournament play that I remember vividly happened in Atlantic City. I was on the 17th hole, underneath a tree, in some deep rough. I had approximately 130 yards to the pin. I wanted a club that would keep it underneath the tree but yet have a little bit of loft to get it out of the deep lie. I moved my hands down on a 7 iron, played the ball back in my stance, and hit the shot within about two feet of the pin. Although my strategy was just to try to get the ball up in front of the green, it actually rolled up a couple of feet from the pin, so it turned out great.

KEY DRILLS FOR FAIRWAY ROUGH SHOTS

Swinging Sensation and Ball Flight Drill

Find some long grass, perhaps on the side of the practice range, and with a 7 iron, take some practice swings. Notice what it feels like when your club is being strangled by the grass. The more familiar you are with the various sensations, the less shock it will be when you're out on the course. Now try to hit a ball out of the rough with your 7 iron. Make the necessary compensations; aim right of your target, open the clubface, open your stance, hinge your wrists early in your backswing, and hold the club slightly firmer than usual. Observe the resulting trajectory. Did the ball tend to go left and low? Did the ball travel a shorter distance than your regular 7 iron? Hit five balls, and see if the ball flight is consistent. If possible, use your 7 iron from different degrees of rough severity, and observe the ball's flights. From extremely severe rough, perhaps you can't advance the ball with this club.

Club-Swapping Drill

Use your pitching wedge, 7 iron, 5 iron, 5 wood, and 3 wood. Place five balls in the rough in similar lies, and use each club to attempt the shot. Observe the ball flight and which club you had the most success with from the lie and which clubs you should not consider using if you are presented with a similar lie on the golf course. Now find a deeper lie in the rough, and repeat the exercise, observing which clubs are successful and which clubs you should not consider from the given lie. Keep trying to find more and more severe rough until you have only one club (pitching wedge) from which you can escape the rough. Caution: be smart and use common sense, as excessive shots in the deep rough can strain muscles.

FAIRWAY ROUGH SUCCESS CHECKLIST

✔ The lie of the ball and your own individual strengths and golfing experience determine your options from the rough. In many instances, you must be realistic, discover the path of least resistance, and choose the shortest way back to the friendly fairway.

✔ The longer and thicker the rough, the more-lofted the club should be. Use more club than you would from the fairway if your lie allows it.

✔ Open your stance and the clubface.

✔ Aim right of your target.

✔ Hold the club slightly firmer than normal, and hinge your wrists earlier on the backswing to encourage a steeper angle of approach.

✔ Because the grass will wrap around the hosel of the club, the ball will tend to go low, left, and shorter but will have more roll than normal.

SUMMARY

Your options in fairway rough are determined by the lie of the ball and your own golfing experience. When the rough is ultrasevere, then the option of taking an unplayable lie is perhaps the smartest of all. It may cost you one stroke, but in the long run, it could save you many more strokes and may protect you from injury. A steeper angle of approach gives you the best opportunity to get the ball to your target. The longer and thicker the rough, the more-lofted the club should be. Open your stance, open the clubface, hold on slightly firmer, and hinge your wrists early on your backswing. Because the grass will be wrapping itself around the neck of your club, your clubhead speed will be reduced, your shot will tend to go left and have less loft and more roll than normal, and your follow-through may be restricted. Understand what to expect when you find your ball in the rough. Find some long grass and practice from it. By knowing what will happen on the course, you can focus on finding the target. Go hit it, hunt it, hole it. Don't let the rough steer you off-course.

Jane Frost, a class A LPGA and PGA professional, is the head professional and director of instruction at Holly Ridge Golf Club. She was the 1994 LPGA National Teacher of the Year and the 1996 New England PGA Teacher of the Year. She has also been named the 1998 PGA Cape Cod Chapter Teacher of the Year. Jane was listed as one of *Golf Magazine*'s Top 100 Teachers in America. She is a past president and three-time tournament champion of the LPGA Teaching and Club Professional Division's Northeast Section. Jane is currently an instructor for the LPGA's National Education Program Series and is a member of the advisory board for Nancy Lopez Golf.

Dottie Pepper was named the 1992 Golf Writers Association Player of the Year and received the 1993 ESPY and Jim Thorpe awards. She won the 1993 World Championship of Women's Golf. In 1999, Dottie won her second major championship at the Nabisco Dinah Shore. She also claimed her 16th career win at the Oldsmobile Classic.

12

Green-Side Rough

Tour Professional: Dottie Pepper
Teaching Professional: Diane McHeffey

The LPGA Tour professionals can get the ball close to the pin from situations that would make many recreational golfers anxious. They are often able to get the ball up-and-down from the green-side rough, when the ball isn't even visible to the spectators. This chapter will help you understand the factors that you must consider when your ball lands in green-side rough. You'll learn what strategy to take and how to execute the shot successfully.

When you find your ball in the green-side rough, the long grass will have a tendency to snag the hosel and decelerate the club or, possibly, close the clubface. The grass caught between the ball and the clubface also reduces the spin that normally would be on the ball. Without the spin, the ball will tend to run more. These factors will help you decide how to approach your shot.

How to Hit Out of Green–Side Rough

SETUP

Use the most-lofted wedge in your bag that will give you the best chance for getting the ball out of the rough. Position the ball farther forward in your stance than normal. For control move your hands down on the grip of the club, effectively reducing the length of the club and creating a shorter arc for shorter distance. Hold the club firmly.

SWING

When the ball is sitting down low in the grass, reduce the amount of grass trapped between the ball and the clubface by producing a more vertical swing plane than in the normal pitch or chip. To achieve a more vertical angle as the clubface descends to the ball, hinge your wrists slightly in the backswing.

How to Hit Out of Green–Side Rough

CONTACT

Swing *through* the ball, staying on the intended target line.

FOLLOW-THROUGH

Maintain balance as you swing to finish.

DOTTIE PEPPER'S GREEN-SIDE ROUGH STRATEGY

First of all, ask yourself these questions before you choose your strategy:

- Must I clear a bunker or obstacle or do I have a straight shot to the green?
- How far is it from the ball to the flagstick?
- How far is it from the edge of the green to the flagstick?
- Am I going to hit uphill? Downhill? Is my lie level with my feet or will my stance be uneven?
- Does the green slope uphill, downhill, or sideways? Does it break or have tiers?

Answers to these questions will determine whether you can carry the ball in the air most of the way to the flag or whether you can hit the ball short and run it up to the flag.

When I'm determining which club to use, I analyze the lie and the distance to the fringe and the hole. I decide how far I must carry the ball. Through experience I understand that the more the ball is buried, the "hotter" the ball will come out with less spin and more roll. When the rough is really long or Bermuda grass, it is harder to predict the trajectory, so I use my most reliable wedge. If the ball is buried in thick grass, I use a technique similar to a bunker shot. I open the clubface and my stance. I swing along my foot line and contact one to two inches behind the ball. The thicker the grass, the more aggressive the swing.

I practice this shot a lot. Because I have confidence in my technique, I trust it, and my focus is always to hole the shot.

OVERCOMING A TOUGH GREEN-SIDE ROUGH SHOT

It was the final round, eighth hole of the 1999 Dinah Shore. The ball was just over the back of the green in the deep rough, about 25 feet from the hole. It was a tough shot, but wiht the use of the sand wedge, I managed to get the ball to 6 feet below the hole. My strategy was just to chop it out and put the ball under the hole. It turned out to be successful!

KEY DRILLS FOR GREEN-SIDE ROUGH SHOTS

Drop-and-Play Drill

Spend time around your practice green hitting shots from different lies in green-side rough. Simply drop the ball and play it as it lies. Do not fluff your ball into a perfect lie. Attempt to hit shots to close and distant holes. Perfect your technique, and focus on solid contact.

Bunker Technique Drill

From the long green-side grass, attempt to hit shots using your bunker technique. Open your stance and your clubface, then take your grip. Play the ball forward in your stance and swing along your body lines, contacting the grass before the ball. Feel like your clubface remains open after contact.

GREEN-SIDE ROUGH SUCCESS CHECKLIST

✔ The longer the grass, the more likely the grass will wrap around the hosel, delofting the club.

✔ The grass trapped between the clubface and the ball will reduce the spin, and the ball will roll more upon landing.

✔ Move your hands down on the club, and hold it slightly firmer than normal.

✔ Place the ball forward in your stance, and hinge your wrists to produce a steeper angle of approach into the ball.

✔ You can successfully play this shot like a green-side bunker shot when the grass is extremely thick. Remember to follow through and accelerate the club through the grass.

✔ Trust your swing and allow the club to propel your ball to your target.

SUMMARY

Successful shots from green-side rough are imperative if you are going to realize your potential. You are going to miss some greens in almost every round. By understanding and adjusting your technique, you can concentrate on your target. Normally you will use your most-lofted club, open your stance and clubface, and position your ball farther forward in your stance to encourage a steeper angle of approach. You may want to move your hands down the club for control and hold the club more firmly to keep the clubface square as the grass wraps around the neck of the club. The more you practice, the more confident you will be—and the more creative you can become from the green-side rough.

Diane McHeffey has been a member of the LPGA's Teaching and Club Professional Division since 1982. She is the owner and director of golf at the Double Tee Golf Center in Hendersonville, North Carolina; a 25-acre teaching complex Diane designed and developed with a driving range, short game practice facility, batting cages, and miniature golf course. She also serves as the executive director for the junior golf program she founded in her area. In 1997, she was honored as both the LPGA Southeast Section Teacher of the Year and the LPGA National Teacher of the Year.

Meg Mallon claimed her first career victory in 1991 at the Oldsmobile LPGA Classic and went on to win the Mazda LPGA Championship, U.S. Women's Open, and the Daikyo World Championship. In 1999, she posted eight top-10 finishes including her 10th and 11th career wins at the Naples LPGA Memorial and the Sara Lee Classic, respectively.

13

Flop Shot

Tour Professional: Meg Mallon
Teaching Professional: Diane McHeffey

The *flop shot*, by definition, is a shot used around the green where you need to produce a very high, soft, arching shot, for example, when the pin is cut close to the edge of the green and you have a bunker, rough, or some other obstacle between you and the green. The flop shot is required when you have very little green to work with and you need to get the ball high in the air quickly so it lands softly with a minimum of roll.

There are some shots that require a certain amount of finesse that only playing experience can provide. The flop shot should only be taken to the course once you have practiced and developed a strong sense of confidence. Although it can sometimes save you strokes, it is a low-percentage shot even for accomplished players.

How to Hit Flop Shots

SETUP

In general, you will use your most-lofted club for this shot. Your stance should be narrow and slightly open. Your ball should be positioned off the inside of your target instep, forward of center. Open the clubface slightly, then place your hands on the club in your normal hold.

SWING

Swing along your body lines. The open stance will create a steeper or more upright swing path than a normal pitch, helping to create height and limit distance. A longer swing will also help send the ball high but not far. On the backswing, hinge your wrists to encourage a steep angle of approach.

How to Hit Flop Shots

CONTACT

On the forward swing, reduce your wrist motion, and do not hinge your wrists after contact. The clubface stays open throughout the swing, and you'll feel like the club is sliding under the ball. Your tempo is the same on your backswing and forward swing—long and rhythmical.

FOLLOW-THROUGH

This shot requires a bigger swing in general, especially on the follow-through.

MEG MALLON'S FLOP SHOT STRATEGY

The flop shot really isn't a high-percentage shot, but sometimes it is the only option if you need to get the ball close to the hole. For example, I use the flop shot when I am in greenside rough with a good lie and with very little green to work with.

I consider the lie of the ball, the height of the obstacle, and the distance to the hole when selecting a club. In general, it's a good idea to use your most-lofted club for this shot. The sand wedge is easier to use than a pitching wedge, because it has more loft. Lob wedges, which have more loft than a sand wedge, are ideal for this shot. I tend to use my high-lofted 60-degree sand wedge.

The flop shot requires 100 percent confidence. If you don't have that kind of confidence, never use it, because a flop shot executed incorrectly can result in a disastrous situation. It is a difficult shot and one that you must really concentrate on and respect. It requires not only good technique but also great feel. The lie has to be just right before I will even consider hitting this shot.

I open my stance, hips, and shoulders. I position the ball forward. (The setup is similar to a bunker shot.) I use a much steeper angle of approach than a regular swing.

AP Photo/Osamu Honda

The flop shot is a difficult shot because of the power needed to get the ball in the air quickly, yet this power (long swing) needs to be tempered by controlling the swing plane angle and contact, which promotes a high, soft shot. The flop shot requires precision, and you should only attempt it when you have a reasonable lie. The tighter your lie, the more challenging the flop shot becomes. When used in appropriate situations, after much practice, it can save you shots.

A WINNING FLOP SHOT

In 1996 in Hawaii, I was in contention and missed the green at the par 5, 15th hole. My competitor was close for birdie. The only way I could get the ball close to save par was to hit a flop shot. I hit the ball two feet from the hole, saved par, and went on to win the 1996 Cup Noodles Hawaiian Ladies Open.

KEY DRILLS FOR FLOP SHOTS

Technique Drill

You must practice the flop shot to be able to execute it with confidence during actual playing conditions. Experimenting is the best way to gain an understanding of how high and soft you can hit shots. First experiment by hitting five balls, opening your stance more on each shot. Next hit five shots, this time opening your clubface more on each shot. Now hit five shots, making each additional swing longer, but at the same pace as the previous shot. Then get creative and try combining the elements of open stance, open clubface, and length of swing to achieve the height and distance you desire.

Strategy Drill

Once you are confident with your technique, practice actual flop shot situations at the practice green where you attempt to carry bunkers, heavy rough, and hills. Try to land the ball softly on a green sloping away from you. Trust that you can produce the trajectory and distance you envision. Once you are confident at the practice tee, you can take the flop shot confidently to the course.

FLOP SHOT SUCCESS CHECKLIST

✔ Use your most-lofted club.

✔ Examine the lie and be confident you can hit a flop shot from the lie.

✔ Position the ball forward in your stance.

✔ Open your clubface, open your stance, and swing along your body line with good rhythm and tempo.

✔ Slide the club under the ball.

✔ Trust your swing.

SUMMARY

Not for the faint of heart, the flop shot is a specialty shot, one of the game's more precise and difficult shots. However, when used in the proper situations, such as in deep green-side rough with a pin cut close to the edge of the green, it can be a score-saver if executed correctly. The flop shot requires controlled yet relaxed power. You must execute enough of a swing to launch the ball quickly with an immediate vertical takeoff, yet controlled enough to limit airborne travel distance to permit a soft landing with almost no roll.

Open your stance, open your clubface, hinge your wrists on the backswing, and minimize your wrist action on the forward swing. Take a long rhythmic swing to produce a high, soft shot. Practice this shot until you are comfortable, then use it on the course when the lie allows and the shot requires a high trajectory and a pillow-soft landing.

Diane McHeffey has been a member of the LPGA's Teaching and Club Professional Division since 1982. She is the owner and director of golf at the Double Tee Golf Center in Hendersonville, North Carolina; a 25-acre teaching complex Diane designed and developed with a driving range, short game practice facility, batting cages, and miniature golf course. She also serves as the executive director for the junior golf program she founded in her area. In 1997, she was honored as both the Southeast Section Teacher of the Year and the LPGA National Teacher of the Year.

PART III

Playing the Game of Golf

Annika Sörenstam won the World Amateur championship in 1992. She was the 1994 Rolex Rookie of the Year and won the Vare Trophy in 1995, 1996, and 1998. Annika also won the 1998 Rolex Player of the Year award for the third time in four years. In 1999, she won twice and brought her career victory total to 18— more than any other tour player in the 1990s. Since winning her first tour title in 1995, Annika has missed only three cuts in 91 starts.

Course Management

Tour Professional: Annika Sörenstam

Course management has to do with developing an overall game strategy. To be successful, you must have a plan for tackling each hole and a strategy for choosing the best routes to the green. You've learned the skills for playing each shot. By coupling these skills with the tips in this chapter, you'll learn how to take the success you've had in practice and carry it with you onto the course.

Pregame Preparation

Whether you're getting ready for a tournament or a casual game with your friends, it helps to go through a few pregame activities in order to familiarize yourself with the course and warm up your body.

Scouting Out the Course

It is important to become familiar with the characteristics of the course before the start of a game or tournament. While some of the specific shot strategy is reserved until actual play, it is still essential to begin with an overall game plan. A day or two before a tournament, my caddie and I will scout out the course. My caddie knows every yardage around the course. When I get to the course, I go out and play. I try to get a feel for what kind of shots I need to play, figure out what places I want to hit the ball and places where I don't want to hit the ball, and see if there are any particular shots that are important around that course. For example, on some courses, it is very important to drive the ball well, so I would work on that before the tournament started. On other courses, it may help to work on some chip shots where there are really tricky greens with big undulations. When I play the course, I'm just trying to get used to the course and figure out what kind of shots I need.

If you're playing a recreational round, many facilities have a detailed score card or yardage book that thoroughly describes course yardage, terrain, hole placement, and even where the flagsticks are placed.

Warming Up

On the day of the tournament, I show up at the golf course about an hour and 15 minutes before I play. I start off with putting. First, I begin with longer putts to try to get a feel around the greens, then I move down to shorter putts. After putting for 15 to 20 minutes, I chip a little bit. I usually begin with a 7 iron and do rolling chips around the green, then go down to a 9 iron, and finish up with a few sand wedges.

After that, I hit some full-swing shots, starting with the sand wedge to warm up. I hit the shorter shots first and end with the driver. Before I leave, I hit some sand wedges again to get the rhythm going. Before I head to the course or to the first tee, I finish with really short putts to boost my confidence before I start.

If you are a recreational player, warming up is also important to get your mind and body ready for the game. Start with short irons, finish with full swings, and always take some putts to get a feel for the green and to finish your practice with confidence. Remember 63 percent of your score is from approach shots to the green (pitching, chipping, and putting), so make sure to practice short shots before you play.

Planning Your Route to the Green

During the game you must also come up with a strategy for playing each hole. The first step is recognizing your own strengths and limitations when it comes to executing certain shots. The second step involves carefully scoping out the hole and noting any potential trouble areas, like sand or water, high roughs, et cetera. From this you can designate certain areas as "safe" places to land the ball. By comparing your strengths and weaknesses to the layout of the hole, you can decide the best path to the green and the club you should use to get it there.

For example, my ultimate goal in the tee shot is to place it well. To do this, I look at the hole in the opposite way—from green to tee. By measuring the shot this way, I can see where I need to be in the fairway to hit the best shot into the green. Sometimes the driver might not be the best club choice. It could be that the driver would carry the shot too far or that it would put the ball at an angle where it couldn't get to the flag. I always plan at least one shot ahead.

From the fairway, if I can't reach the green in two on a par 5, I always lay up to my favorite distance, which is 80 yards. My caddie counts back how far I have to hit the ball to leave it 80 yards from the flag. To get there on a par 5, most often my second shot is a 7 or 5 wood. From 80 yards, I usually hit a lob wedge, depending on the conditions. This is a strategy that you could also adopt, according to the distance that works best for you.

Club selection varies when the distance is in between clubs. It depends so much on where the flagstick is. For example, if the pin is toward the front of the green and I'm in between clubs, I like to get the ball on the green. So in that case, I would put the ball past the pin. If the pin is in the back of the green and I'm in between, then I'd rather be short just to make sure the ball gets on the green.

In general, I'm a fast player, and I don't like slow play. I think a lot of golfers tend to take too much time reading putts, figuring out the wind, and calculating the yardage. I personally think that once you calculate the yardage, there are not that many shots to choose from. Try to make it simple. Try to hit a good shot and always try to curve it less—the less time you have to think about what kind of shot to hit, the better your shot will most likely be.

The Mental Game

You've studied the course, developed a general game plan, and primed your body for play. Now it's time to hit the course. You now have a chance to put your skills together and apply what you've learned. The physical aspect of golf, however, is not the only factor in determining success. One of the biggest challenges, whether you're competing against yourself or in a major tournament, is the mental game of golf. The way you react to a bad shot, the mindset you have during your pre-swing routine, and your thoughts in between shots are all factors that can make or break your game.

Maintaining Focus and Composure

It's very important to get eye concentration on the shot, focusing 100 percent on the target and the shot you are about to make. The only thing you should think about is what you are going to do right at that particular moment. Have positive thoughts and just focus on what you need to do. If you happen to hit a shot you don't really like, try to get over it as soon as possible. The quicker you can forget about that shot, the better you're going to do on the next one. Just try to get your mind focused on something else. When you're in between shots, think of different things so that you save your energy for when it's time to hit. When it comes time for the next shot, don't think about the last shot— just go up there and try to hit a good shot again.

I always try to keep my thoughts on the shot at hand.

Staying Positive

Whether or not you've just had a great first round or a not-so-great round, the key to keeping your momentum up is to stay positive. When the day starts, you've just got to have positive thoughts. Go out there and remember the best round you ever played. Try to have good thoughts around the greens and when you tee up. If you get off to a good start, then I hope you'll have a lot of confidence, which will carry through to the next shot. If you don't have a good round, simply put it behind you and strive for a good shot on the next one. Always try to remember the good shots that you've played to stay positive.

Playing Your Own Game

To avoid feeling pressured by the play of others, it's very important to play your own game. By this I mean you must hit your shots and the shots that you know how to hit. Hit one shot at a time and focus on your game only. I don't really look at other players when they swing or putt, so I don't get any images of something that could interrupt my focus or composure. I just want to try to remember my good shots and focus on my game, not somebody else's.

Different Variables in Golf

Even when you've gone great lengths to prepare yourself both mentally and physically for a game, there are still times when the unexpected and uncontrollable happens. Rain delays and extreme temperatures are just two variables that will sometimes try to wreak havoc on your game and concentration. The following are ways to help you stay positive and focused when confronted with these situations.

Rain Delays

There is nothing you can do about rain delays or some other types of delays. You've just got to deal with it. Try to stay relaxed, talk about things other than golf, and try to not think too much on your round. Again, you want to save the energy for the next few rounds you're going to play, assuming it's the same day, so try to stay focused on other things and play golf when you get out there.

Extreme Temperatures

It's very important to drink water, of course. Try to stay away from the sun. If you have an umbrella, use it. Try to go in the shade as much as possible and avoid quick motions. Walk slowly; take your time. If your

To avoid the pressures and distractions around me, I concentrate on my game and not that of my competitors.

hands sweat, just use a towel to dry them off so they don't slip. Again, it is very important to drink water during the round and also before the round.

I enjoy challenging courses that require you to hit every club in the bag. Therefore, I recognize the importance of course management. Without a strategy for getting the ball from tee to green, you will never feel in control of your game. You must gauge your abilities against each particular shot and plan a pathway to the hole. With a plan of attack, positive attitude, and focused mind, you'll be in complete control!

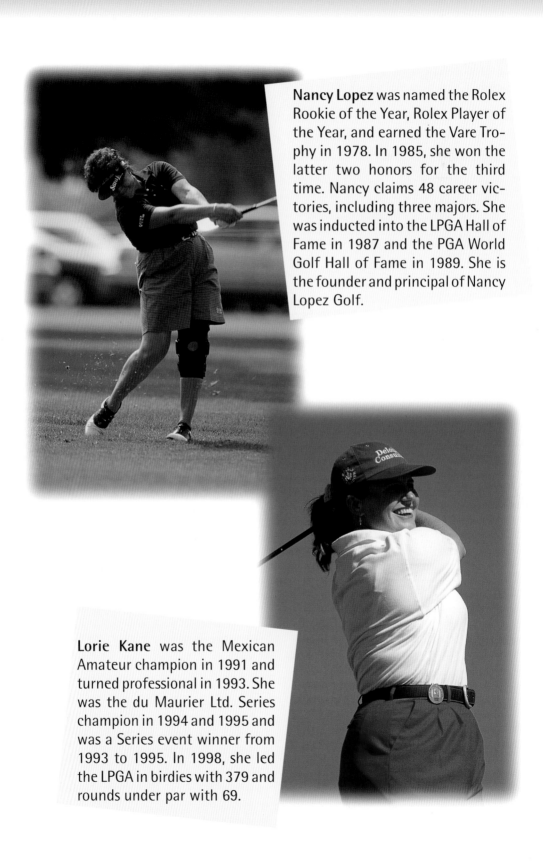

Nancy Lopez was named the Rolex Rookie of the Year, Rolex Player of the Year, and earned the Vare Trophy in 1978. In 1985, she won the latter two honors for the third time. Nancy claims 48 career victories, including three majors. She was inducted into the LPGA Hall of Fame in 1987 and the PGA World Golf Hall of Fame in 1989. She is the founder and principal of Nancy Lopez Golf.

Lorie Kane was the Mexican Amateur champion in 1991 and turned professional in 1993. She was the du Maurier Ltd. Series champion in 1994 and 1995 and was a Series event winner from 1993 to 1995. In 1998, she led the LPGA in birdies with 379 and rounds under par with 69.

Life and Golf

Tour Professionals: Nancy Lopez and Lorie Kane

As anyone who has played knows, golf is a great recreational and competitive sport for men and women at any age. The class and courtesy that the game demands are just two values that can be carried over into everyday life. Being outdoors, smelling the fresh air, and enjoying the physical benefits of the game have turned many skeptics into lifelong golfers. The challenge for some, however, lies in finding time in their busy lives to play the game. Two of the sport's finest—Nancy Lopez and Lorie Kane—offer advice on making golf a part of your life.

Giving Everything 100 Percent
Nancy Lopez

Golf is a great sport. It gets you out into the fresh air where you can leave behind everyday worries and frustrations that come from having to juggle career, family, friends, et cetera. It's a game that everyone can play. Just go out there and have fun, enjoy a beautiful day, and forget about the frustrations of life. You don't need to have mastered every shot in this book; in fact, part of the fun of golf is learning to hit those shots. When you practice and you learn what you can do with your swing and your shot-making ability, that's the fun of it.

If you tend to get frustrated with golf, stop and put everything in perspective. It's just a game. And if you allow yourself the chance to treat it as such, you'll realize that it's fun to simply be out there hitting balls and enjoying a walk among the birds, the sky, and the breeze.

Fitting Golf Into Your Life

With the demands of everyday life, it's difficult to find time to relax and enjoy a game of golf. The demands of having a career and family make it seemingly impossible to schedule time for yourself. The way I've been able to handle everything that's going on in my life is by giving 100 percent to whatever I'm doing. When I'm playing golf, I give it 100 percent. I don't really think about anything else except golf at that time. When I'm with my kids, I give them 100 percent, and when I'm with my husband, I give him 100 percent. Sometimes it's hard to do that, but it's just a matter of making the best of your time.

When I'm on the course, 100 percent of my focus and attention goes to my game.

I also think that organization is very important. By preparing for the day and setting a schedule, you'll be making smart use of your time, and it will be much easier to fit a game of golf into your day.

Rebounding From Setbacks

Whenever I experience a setback in my game, I remind myself that I'm so lucky to play golf and be able to do what I'm doing. I've had a lot of positive things happen in my life and in my career. If you're down and having a bad day, it sometimes helps to look at the good things that have happened in your life and set aside those feelings of frustration.

It is also my faith and my family that really help me get through setbacks. I know that God is there and He will help me and encourage me anyway that He can. Plus, I have a family and a husband that constantly support and encourage me. Sometimes setbacks are easier to deal with when you have somebody there that you can share your thoughts and feelings with.

It's important to understand that you can't carry your golf home with you. Play it and leave it at the course. If you don't play well, forget it and come back tomorrow and do a better job.

A Lifelong Pursuit

You can pursue golf at any age. I started when I was eight by following my mom and dad around the golf course, and I loved it. I think children should be encouraged to play. Let them try it, and if they don't like it then, just let them back away until they're ready to do it again. If you take them out there with you on the golf course a lot, they'll get the bug, and they'll want to play with you. We've never forced our kids to play golf. We would simply like them to play for the fun and recreation of it.

I definitely encourage anybody who wants to play to start at any age. I've seen people become golfers at ages well over 50 who have just loved it.

Golf is something you can do all your life. It's not hard on the body like other sports can be. Swinging keeps your muscles limber. Walking keeps your heart healthy and your legs strong. This is important to me especially now that I realize how bad my knees are. If I hadn't been working out and walking, my knees would probably be in much worse shape than they are now.

I look forward to playing golf with my kids for a long, long time. Hopefully, they'll find an interest in golf and play for fun. I don't particularly care if they turn professional. I just want them to enjoy golf and have fun with it, and I encourage you to do the same.

Finding Time for What You Love
Lorie Kane

I turned pro at the age of 29 in 1993, but golf has always been something I enjoyed doing, and I always found time to do it. For those players who balance work and children, but still want to be able to enjoy the great sport of golf, my advice is to set priorities. Obviously, if I was a mother, my children would be a priority, and if I had a job outside of golf, that would also be a priority. In those cases, golf would have to come second. But when you love a sport, you'll always find a place for it. Even if it's only nine holes in the evening, that's still nine holes in which you can enjoy the fresh air and a walk around a beautiful golf course. When you've given yourself a couple of hours of your own time to enjoy a great game of golf, it will likely make you that much more sharp when you head home to the kids or back to the office.

Overcoming Frustration

When you happen to hit a bad shot or you're having an off day on the course, you can only be your own best friend. Those words came to me from a Canadian pro by the name of Moe Norman, and I take that advice with me. To overcome frustration, just enjoy the game and make light of the situation—this goes for both competitive and recreational players. The first time I went to Japan to play in the Japan Classic, I took great comfort in seeing how the Japanese approach the game. If they hit a bad shot, they laughed and left it behind them and focused on the next hole.

Learning Valuable Lessons

I believe that golf is the only game of honor that's left. In competitive and recreational golf, it's you the player who will call yourself if a rule is breached. In everyday life, it's sometimes hard to confront these issues. However, golf teaches you a discipline and honesty that will carry over into your everyday life.

In golf the challenge lies between you and the golf course, whereas in other sports it's usually you and the opposing team or the person you're playing against. If you can go out, enjoy yourself, and work hard to beat the golf course, then at the end of the day, you'll have success.

Whether you're a long-time golfer or a beginning player, remember to take a moment on the course and enjoy your surroundings. Relax, set up the shot, take a swing, and leave behind the frustrations of your day. Relishing the moment will not only make you more successful in golf but also in life.

About the LPGA

The Ladies Professional Golf Association (LPGA) is dedicated to the worldwide promotion and advancement of women's golf. The LPGA is committed to advancing women and the sport of golf through expanding its Tournament Division, its Teaching and Club Professional (T&CP) Division, and The LPGA Foundation programs, the LPGA's charitable arm.

The LPGA also provides additional opportunites to bring people into the game, including the LPGA Urban Youth Program, LPGA Girls Golf Club, The Ronald McDonald House Charities LPGA Tour Junior Golf Clinics, and the LPGA Golf Clinics for Women. Through its tournaments, more than $102 million has been raised for local charities from 1981 to 1999.

Founded in 1950, the LPGA is headquartered in Daytona Beach, Florida, at LPGA International, which houses the association's home golf course. The oldest, longest running women's professional sports organization in the world, the LPGA celebrates its 50th anniversary in 2000.

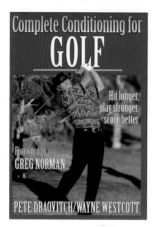

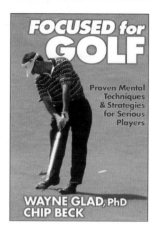

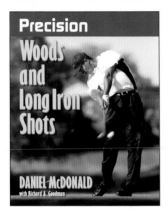

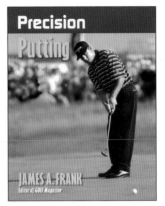